Prais

FIND
OUR VOICE

"I want to shout, 'Finally!' At last, we have a book that discusses contextualized preaching among Asian North Americans while upholding the authority of Scripture. Matthew Kim and Daniel Wong are eminently qualified to offer a practical and culturally aware guide to the particularities of Asian North American hermeneutics, theology, and pulpit. This is a much-needed book that should be welcome in both the church and the classroom."

—Daniel K. Eng, instructor, Moody Theological Seminary,
and affiliated lecturer, University of Cambridge

"What an important contribution Kim and Wong give us to the pastoral and preaching worlds through *Finding Our Voice*. This book gives an insightful look at our past, seeing what shaped and influenced our Asian North American spirituality, what the current challenges are today, and most importantly how we can effectively preach to and minister to Asian North Americans in our congregations going forward. This book is not only for Asian pastors or Asian congregations, but for any pastor who has Asians in their church. There is wisdom to be gained through reading this book, and the fruit of it will be effective gospel ministry as we apply it."

—Eddie Byun, associate professor of Christian ministry,
Talbot School of Theology

"Who are Asian North American (ANA) preachers? What do sermons shaped by and attuned to ANA stories and values distinctly sound like? Who are ANA congregations? Questions like these are seldom explored systematically or in depth, as Matthew Kim and Daniel Wong do in this book. *Finding Our Voice* is a gift that reminds ANA preachers of the value of our ethnic heritages and multicultural identities in proclaiming the gospel, even if experiences of pain and disorientation color our stories. Regardless of their racial and ethnic background, I recommend this resource to all preachers who sincerely want to understand and reach ANA listeners with the life-giving news of Jesus Christ, who loves us for who we are."

—Ahmi Lee, assistant professor of preaching,
Fuller Theological Seminary

"This book provides a much-needed stepping stone for the further development of the distinctive voices and contributions that Asian North American preachers can be making. While preaching to a generic audience can be edifying, preaching and teaching to a specific Asian North American culture can be transformative all the more."

—DJ Chuang, author of *MultiAsian.Church:*
A Future for Asian Americans in a Multiethnic World

"*Finding Our Voice* hails the significant voices of Asian Americans who seek to live out the gospel and preach as minorities in a Eurocentric society. The book extends far beyond Asian American history, culture, church, and theology, with its intricate inclusion of models of prophetic preaching. *Finding Our Voice* is a significant book for spiritual minds and proves itself to be essential for our time."

—Grace Ji-Sun Kim, associate professor of theology,
Earlham School of Religion, and author of *Reimagining Spirit*

"*Finding Our Voice* is a very helpful and well-written book describing a vision for Asian North American preaching. It includes excellent and concise overviews of the Asian North American experience, hermeneutics, theology, and preaching, both now and in the future. It is a must-read not only for Asian North American Christians—especially pastors and church leaders—but also for all Christians."

—Siang-Yang Tan, professor of psychology, Fuller
Theological Seminary; senior pastor, First Evangelical Church,
Glendale, California; author of *Shepherding God's People* and
Counseling and Psychotherapy: A Christian Perspective

"*Finding Our Voice* is a tremendous contribution to the field of homiletics and to the body of Christ. Now that Matthew Kim and Daniel Wong have found their voices, this exemplary treatise guides us in finding ours. In this didactic, interactive, inspiring, and empowering volume, we are trained by two brilliant scholar/practitioners in how to preach the immutable gospel of a global Jesus through our God-given ethnic identities and cultural narratives. Written for the Asian North American (ANA) context, this work will not only help readers find our voice; it also teaches us how to hear the voices of our beloved neighbors. This is a must read!"

—Emmett G. Price III, professor of worship, church, and culture
and executive director, Institute for the Study of the Black Christian
Experience, Gordon-Conwell Theological Seminary

"Phenotypes matter! If evangelicals might think that focusing on our raciality or ethnicity kowtows to the identity politics of a liberal or progressive agenda, Matthew Kim and Daniel Wong are prophets who call attention to the incarnational character of the gospel manifest historically in and through many cultures and languages. We 1.5-generation, second-generation, and later members of Asian North American communities need to find our voice in this regard—precisely because we look and sound different. I hope that Kim and Wong's prophetic proclamation will find a hearing among many of our pastors, leaders, and congregations who live perpetually in foreign spaces."

—Amos Yong, professor of theology and mission
and dean, School of Theology and School of
Intercultural Studies, Fuller Theological Seminary

"Matthew Kim and Daniel Wong have done a great service to the North American Christian church, evangelicals in particular, by stepping into the often-overlooked arena of Asian North American preaching. They have provided us with a resource book that is visionary and thought-provoking. Bible teachers and preachers, new and old, will be helped by the conversations they spark and the questions they raise. They are spot-on in their naming of the common Asian North American experience and narrative, as well as considering core hermeneutics that acknowledge the bicultural/multicultural/both-and background of Asian North American preachers and peoples. I can hardly wait for *Finding Our Voice* to be used by hermeneutical communities within churches, seminaries, and marketplaces."

—Donna Dong, multiethnic/multicultural ministry director,
InterVarsity Christian Fellowship of Canada

"Matthew Kim and Daniel Wong have provided a desperately needed resource in our rapidly emerging post-Christendom and multicultural world. In our attempts to understand the missional contexts of neighborhoods, we have tended to focus superficially on 'food, fashion, and festival,' missing the opportunity to move deeper into the intercultural possibilities in this new world of diversity. To preach in this new world requires an understanding that allows the word to come alive. To do so, however, requires a sensitivity to the shades of difference—so that the differences come alive to the possibilities of faith and discipleship. Kim and Wong have given us a gift if we want to learn to preach multiculturally. It will change the way we think about preaching."

—Gary V. Nelson, president, Tyndale University,
home of Tyndale Seminary

"I've been hoping and praying for the day when most Asian North American (ANA) seminary students and many ANA pastors will be clamoring to become culturally embodied, contextually attuned, and compellingly perceptive ANA preachers. Now that Daniel Wong and Matthew Kim have carefully researched and written this book, there's finally a requisite resource to answer their questions and to launch them on this journey, one that I have been waiting on for more than forty years."

—Ken Fong, host of *Asian America: The Ken Fong Podcast*
and author of *Secure in God's Embrace* and *Pursuing the Pearl*

"Matthew Kim and Daniel Wong have put together an indispensable resource for all Asian North American preachers and pastors. *Finding Our Voice* brings together the latest and best resources to help shape a contextualized Asian North American hermeneutic, theology, and preaching presentation. I commend these authors for their invaluable contribution to a global audience, giving us a preview of a future Revelation 5 and 7 congregation."

—Benjamin S. Shin, associate professor of Christian ministry
and leadership, Talbot School of Theology, Biola University

"Matthew Kim and Daniel Wong captured my attention with *Finding Our Voice*. Their transparency intrigued me not only with their candor through transparency, but through their skillful selection of words that described my feelings. This won my openness to consider their thinking on the implications of a mono-theology that is too quickly assumed by many in our field. I like a book that posits a new way of thinking that is better than the status quo. Suggestions of a hybrid hermeneutic or an incarnational duality left me wondering and pondering. I liked this read and recommend it to you."

—Bruce Fong, professor of pastoral ministries,
Dallas Theological Seminary

FINDING OUR VOICE

FINDING OUR VOICE

A Vision for Asian North American Preaching

Matthew D. Kim & Daniel L. Wong

Foreword by Ken Shigematsu

LEXHAM PRESS

Finding Our Voice: A Vision for Asian North American Preaching

Copyright 2020 Matthew D. Kim and Daniel L. Wong

Lexham Press, 1313 Commercial St., Bellingham, WA 98225
LexhamPress.com

Print ISBN: 9781683593782
Digital ISBN: 9781683593799
Library of Congress Control Number: 2020931314

Lexham Editorial Team: Elliot Ritzema, Allisyn Ma, Jessi Strong, David Bomar
Cover Design: Jim LePage
Typesetting: Justin Marr

To Ryan, Evan, and Aidan—
May you embrace your Korean American identity
and embody your Christian identity to the glory of God.
—Matthew D. Kim

To my wife, Flora, for her loving support and encouragement
and to our children, Joshua and Tiffany,
for the way you bring perspective, hope, and love
to your own and future generations.
—Daniel L. Wong

CONTENTS

ACKNOWLEDGMENTS

This book was in search of a publishing home until Jim Weaver shared our vision to publish it for the Asian North American church and beyond. Thank you, Jim, for believing in this project. Thanks to the wonderful team at Lexham Press, including Abby Salinger and Elliot Ritzema, for their diligence, guidance, and encouragement throughout the process. And thanks to Ken Shigematsu for writing an insightful foreword.

I want to thank Gordon-Conwell Theological Seminary for their generous sabbatical program. Thanks, in particular, to my preaching colleagues, Jeffrey Arthurs, Patricia Batten, and Pablo Jiménez for covering various responsibilities during the spring of 2019. Thanks to Daniel for writing this book with me. Your wisdom and experience in the Asian North American context are greatly appreciated. Thanks to my parents, Ki Wang and Taek Hee Kim, and my in-laws, Chung Hyun and Jung Sook Oh, for their constant encouragement. I also want to express appreciation to my wife, Sarah, who provides ample space for me to preach, teach, and write. Thank you, and I love you. And to my three sons, Ryan, Evan, and Aidan, you have sacrificed a lot in being the son of a pastor and seminary professor. It's my honor to dedicate this book to you. Remember always that the most important thing in life is loving Jesus. I am so proud to be your father. Above all, I give thanks and glory to our triune God: Father, Son, and Holy Spirit.

—Matthew

I had many people who were instrumental in facilitating both knowledge and experience for me to write my portion of this book. I am grateful to my past teachers of preaching, including: Haddon Robinson, Donald Sunukjian, John Reed, David Larsen, Stephen Farris, Arthur Van Seters, and Paul Scott Wilson. Many congregations in Canada and in the United States experienced my preaching and gave helpful feedback. I cherish the fellowship and robust discussions about Asian North American ministry and preaching I've had with the English Speaking Chinese Ministerial and the Pastors' Fellowship Network, both in Toronto. My students at Tyndale University (formerly Tyndale University College & Seminary), where I have taught preaching since 1997, continually challenge my thinking about preaching.

I am grateful to Matthew for inviting me to co-write this book. His skill at writing and navigating the publishing world is amazing. He was always patient and gracious to me. Marilyn Law served as an editor for me. She pays close attention to details, asks great questions, and provides comments. She is a second-generation, Canadian-born Chinese and a member of my previous congregation. Marilyn spent a number of years in the United States, so she can see both sides of the Canadian/American border. Some of the unsung heroes are members of the Tyndale University's undergraduate faculty prayer group. They regularly prayed for me to meet the interim deadlines and checked on me regularly.

Ultimately, the Lord Jesus Christ is to be thanked for providing strength to complete the task (Phil 4:13; Acts 20:24). He is the one who gives substance and voice to my life, ministry, and preaching.

—Daniel

FOREWORD

I was sitting alone on one side of a long rectangular table in a board-room of one of Tokyo's landmark corporate towers. It was a final job interview for a promising position in this company. Sitting on the other side of the table were four people: three managers and an administrative assistant who sat off to the far right. The manager in the middle of the group was a man in his fifties. He had a stout build, a square jaw, and a husky voice—a Japanese version of Jack Nicholson.

"If we hire you," he rasped, "how long would you stay with our company?"

I paused and said, "Not that long. Maybe two or three years?"

"Why not longer?" he asked.

"I want to one day enter the Christian ministry and work as a pastor."

The manager furrowed his brow with incredulity, leaned in, and growled, "Why would you want to do *that*?" My heart began to beat faster, my mind went blank, and I mumbled something along the lines of, "I think it would be the best way for me to serve people."

Riding home on the subway after the interview, I reflected on this question and realized my answer was incomplete: I wasn't inter-ested in Christian ministry simply because I wanted to *serve people*;

I wanted to do something in my life that would *last forever*. For me, that meant serving as a pastor.

Of course, you don't need to enter into full-time pastoral ministry to make your life count. God can use countless vocations to fulfill his purposes.

However, if you have been called to preach the word, in a very direct way, you are doing something that will last forever. As you preach, lives are transformed and destinies are altered.

It may well be that when you first spoke about your decision to enter into vocational Christian ministry there were people in your life (like the manager at the company where I was applying for a job) who furrowed their brows in disapproval or even vehemently objected. But know that you are doing something extremely challenging and also truly glorious and eternally significant. In losing your life for this call, you will find it.

In *Finding Our Voice*, my friends, Matthew Kim and Daniel Wong, will help you hear again the incomparable voice that first called you into the lifework in which you find yourself engaged. This book will give you a fresh sense of the glory of your preaching vocation.

As the title suggests, this work aims to help you find your unique voice as an Asian preacher (or for those who preach to people from Asian ancestries).

During my seminary years, I did a summer internship in Singapore to help lay the groundwork for an evangelistic campaign at the National Stadium where Leighton Ford, the brother-in-law and long-time senior associate of Billy Graham, was going to preach. Part of my role was preaching in some of the churches in Singapore.

After one of my sermons, I had a feeling that an elder at one of the churches was a little disappointed that Leighton Ford Ministries hadn't arranged for a preacher from the Southern part of the United States, who might have resembled more closely a tall, commanding, Caucasian like Billy Graham or Leighton Ford.

I blurted out an unsolicited apology: "I know [as a younger, Asian person] I probably wasn't what you were expecting. You were probably hoping for someone older, whiter, wearing a white, double-breasted suit, preaching in a Southern accent."

The older Asian man smiled and said, "Actually, we weren't expecting Colonel Sanders to show up. We're glad you're here. We just want you to be you."

Perhaps, at times, you have wanted to be someone that you're not (maybe a Caucasian or African American preacher you admire).

Matthew and Daniel will help you not only find your voice, but preach powerfully as you embrace the unique strengths of your cultural heritage. You may never preach like a John Piper or a T. D. Jakes, but no one can preach like you in your uniqueness. As visible minorities living a bicultural existence, Matthew and Daniel help us discover the unique beauty and power of our ethnic heritage and connect this to our call. To echo the words of the jazz musician Duke Ellington, they will help you "become a number one yourself, rather than a number two somebody else."

As you turn the following pages, read prayerfully, open your heart, and receive anew God's call to proclaim Christ as only you can.

Ken Shigematsu
Pastor of Tenth Church, Vancouver, British Columbia
Author of *Survival Guide for the Soul*

Matthew D. Kim and Daniel L. Wong

PREFACE

The sixth grade commences an unquestionably awkward time in any maturing boy's life. It was during this precarious season that I (Matthew, a second-generation, American-born Korean) learned this sometimes hard to swallow, but very necessary, life lesson about living in the United States: I was not white.

Prior to this epiphany, I had grown up in Park Ridge, a suburb of Chicago, where my brothers and I were oblivious to this as one of two Asian families in our town. My younger brothers, Timothy and Dennis, and I naturally identified as being white. The only people we knew in school and in our neighborhood were white kids. My best friend, Nicky, was white. We spoke English with a standard, white, Midwestern accent, played white sports, and had crushes on white girls. We were white, or so we thought.

After my fifth-grade year, however, our parents moved us seventeen miles northwest to Palatine, Illinois, so that they could live closer to their dry cleaning business and transition us into a higher-quality school district. Post-relocation, my perception of my identity slowly began to shift. I noticed fellow Asians like Koreans, Chinese, Japanese, Indians, Filipinos, and others in our middle school and high school who looked more like my siblings and me. My brain slowly transformed as I witnessed a new reality of a Korean American existence. It became increasingly clear that I was not white. In fact, I was a strange hybrid of American and Korean. I was not either one exclusively; I was both/and.

To be both American and Korean required a new identity. I discovered that I couldn't self-identify as Caucasian. My countenance and physical features were unlike those of my white friends. My father awakened me to this reality when he had me look in the mirror one day, asking, "What do you see?" He answered his own question: "To the dominant culture, you're Korean, and you'll always be Korean." Yet the breakdowns in my ability to feel completely at home in the Korean language and cultural context simultaneously exposed an inability to self-identify as entirely Korean. Rather, I was a strange mixture of American and Korean. Over time, I began to appreciate the ability to eat pizza one evening and kimchi and ramen on another. I could converse in English at school and communicate in my very limited Korean at home to my grandmother and parents.

Today, living on the North Shore of Boston in a very white New England suburb, I sadly continue to face bouts of insecurity. I sometimes still feel a sense of shame for being Asian and wish that I was white. Shortly after moving here, I heard a mocking voice shout out *konnichiwa* ("hello" in Japanese) from a neighbor's window while I was walking down the street. When I spoke back to him in perfect English, he kept repeating *konnichiwa* in a fake, exaggerated Asian accent. This experience of being called out for my difference reminded me of my youth in Park Ridge. However, I try to remind myself that I needn't be embarrassed for being ethnically Korean or for my skin color. In many ways, what I want to communicate in this book is that God desires for us Asian North Americans (ANAs) to celebrate our hybrid, hyphenated, both/and, bicultural, liminal, or perhaps even third-culture self-confidence—a distinct voice and experience reserved by God just for people like me and perhaps you.

My (Daniel's) story is similar, but also different from Matthew's. I was born a third-generation Chinese in San Francisco and raised in Oakland, California. As one of the few Asian Americans in my elementary school, echoes of "Ching-Chong Chinaman" are engraved on my heart and mind. My parents took my older brother and me weekly to a Chinese church in San Francisco's Chinatown in my formative years. I vividly recall sitting in worship services where the preacher would preach in Cantonese, which I did not understand. The sermon would be translated into English by someone with such a thick Chinese accent that I couldn't understand that either. Ventures into Chinatown were scary. Strangers chided my parents that their children didn't speak Chinese. I am sure I received looks of horror when I poured sugar into my Chinese tea. After various negative experiences from inside and even outside the Chinese community, I would cry out to God, "Why didn't you make me one way or the other?" I look Asian, but I feel Caucasian. Some use the term "banana" to describe people like me: one who is yellow on the outside but white on the inside.

My journey swung from loathing my Chinese heritage to embracing it. I eventually found my roots. I took my first Chinese language lessons in college and enrolled in courses like "The Relationship between the US and China" as well as "Chinese Arts and History." In retrospect, I can see how God used some of these experiences to shape my perspective on life, ministry, and preaching. My both/and existence equips me to serve in a both/and world. Particularly, I appreciate the body of Christ analogy, where each person can have and express gifts with a different culture, language, and experience while being a part of the whole.

PREACHING AND ANA IDENTITY

How do these self-revelations relate to the matter of preaching? Every preacher possesses an identity and communicates out of his or her identity. If you were driving your car and surfing stations, you might stumble upon some different radio preachers. Most of us can distinguish between preachers from African American, Hispanic American, and European American backgrounds based on their distinct preaching traditions, styles, accents, and cultural traits. However, could the same be said of Asian North American (ANA) preachers? Do ANA preachers have a preaching voice? Is there anything that makes ANA preachers and ANA preaching distinct? How does our preaching reflect our both/and identity? What does ANA preaching look like today, and what could it look like in the future? These are the questions at the heart of this book.

We contend that ANA preachers are in need of a unique homiletical voice akin to other minority groups such as African American and Hispanic American preaching traditions. Preaching to listeners who embrace this both/and identity as ANAs requires apt contextualization with a culturally aware hermeneutic and homiletic. For this reason, we seek to name the hermeneutical, theological, and homiletical distinctives of ANA preaching in order to help preachers understand the specific characteristics and challenges that distinguish preaching in ANA contexts.

In order to clarify how to preach to ANAs, first we need to clarify what it means to be ANA, for that term encompasses a diverse group. Much of the literature uses the term "Asian American" to refer to those who emigrated from Asia or who are people of Asian descent born and raised in the United States. The term was coined by the historian and activist Yuji Ichioka and was "initially used to describe a politically charged group identity in ethnic consciousness movements of the late 1960s."[1] While this is a convenient and recognized term, few identify themselves as generically Asian or Asian American.

---

1   Min Zhou and Jennifer Lee, "Introduction: The Making of Culture, Identity, and Ethnicity among Asian American Youth," in *Asian American Youth: Culture, Identity and Ethnicity*, ed. Jennifer Lee and Min Zhou (New York: Routledge, 2004), 11. See also Andrea Bittle, "I Am Asian American: Uncover the True Diversity beneath the Asian American Label," *Teaching Tolerance*, vol. 44 (Summer 2013), https://www.tolerance.org/magazine/summer-2013/i-am-asian-american.

Most identify with their ancestral country of origin or ethnic group and their current country of residence (e.g., Chinese American), especially for the second generation and beyond.

The term "Asian North American" has more recently been adopted by social scientists to identify those of Asian descent living in the United States or Canada. Unlike the older concept of "Asian American," "'Asian North American' is a more useful umbrella term because Asian subjects who reside in the United States and in Canada face many of the same issues regarding identity, multiple cultural allegiances, marginalization vis-à-vis mainstream society, historical exclusion, and postcolonial and/or diasporic and/or transnational subjectivity."[2] A number of Christian authors have also taken up this newer nomenclature to describe those born and raised in North America whose parents and ancestors are from Asian countries.[3]

Along with a few others from Canada, Daniel was once invited to take part in a consultation at Trinity Evangelical Divinity School outside Chicago. He learned from this consultation that issues faced by ANA churches were similar whether one resided and ministered in the United States or Canada. There were also unique issues facing each congregation related to the geographic locale, the history of the group, and other factors. He came away with a greater awareness of the need to collaborate across congregations and learn with and from the larger family of ANA churches.

Within the broad category of ANAs, there are two distinct subgroups: "(1) first-generation Asian [North] Americans, that is, foreign-born Asian immigrants and refugees, and (2) second- and

---

2   Eleanor Ty and Donald C. Goellnicht, "Introduction" in *Asian North American Identities: Beyond the Hyphen*, ed. Eleanor Ty and Donald C. Goellnicht (Bloomington, IN: Indiana University Press, 2004), 2.

3   These include David Ng, ed., *People on the Way: Asian North Americans Discovering Christ, Culture, and Community* (Valley Forge, PA: Judson, 1996); Russell Yee, *Worship on the Way: Exploring Asian North American Christian Experience* (Valley Forge, PA: Judson, 2012); and M. Sydney Park, Soong-Chan Rah, and Al Tizon, eds., *Honoring the Generations: Learning from Asian North American Congregations* (Valley Forge, PA: Judson, 2012).

multi-generational US-born [or Canadian-born] Asian [North] Americans."[4] Some have used the label "Asian American" to describe predominantly those in the first generation. A preaching book from a first-generation immigrant's perspective is Eunjoo Mary Kim's *Preaching the Presence of God: A Homiletic from an Asian American Perspective.*[5] This book is helpful for understanding immigrants' experiences, in particular with reference to Korean preaching.

The focus of our book, however, is on the second category of ANAs: English-speaking, second- and multi-generational, US- and Canadian-born Asian North Americans. Further, because of our own experience in these contexts, we will primarily address those from East Asian backgrounds like our own, namely ethnic Koreans and Chinese. However, we hope that other ANAs will find we are describing their experiences as well.

THE NEED FOR ANA VOICES

This book arose from a deep burden for the ANA church and for its future vitality. We saw a dearth of literature on preaching to English-speaking ANAs, and so we decided to step into this gap. Over the years, we have found that many ANA pastors have not considered the ethnicity of themselves and their listeners with respect to their preaching and the uniqueness of what it means to preach to ANAs in a full-orbed sense. Rather, many ANA preachers sound "white," whether intentionally or not, because they write sermons that speak to the "generic American" based on the homiletical instruction they have received in Bible colleges and seminaries from European American preaching professors.[6] We believe that ANA preachers

---

4   Matthew D. Kim, "Asian-American Preaching," in *The Art and Craft of Biblical Preaching: A Comprehensive Resource for Today's Communicators*, ed. Craig Brian Larson and Haddon Robinson (Grand Rapids: Zondervan, 2005), 200. See also http://www.census.gov.

5   Eunjoo Mary Kim, *Preaching the Presence of God: A Homiletic from an Asian American Perspective* (Valley Forge, PA: Judson, 1999).

6   See Matthew D. Kim, *Preaching to Second Generation Korean Americans: Towards a Possible Selves Contextual Homiletic* (New York: Peter Lang, 2007), 1.

require a contextual homiletic that speaks to the bicultural and even multicultural needs of ANA listeners. In short, the ANA church needs its own distinct preaching voice. We seek to find and shape our unique voice in the world of homiletics.

We are not alone in recognizing this perspectival shift and the need for ANA voices. The evangelical Christian movement is sensing this ripe and necessary transformation in leadership as well. We are slowly witnessing the emergence of ANAs embracing international Christian leadership positions as evidenced by Michael Oh becoming the Global Executive Director/CEO of the Lausanne Movement, Tom Lin's presidential selection to lead InterVarsity Christian Fellowship, and Sharon Koh taking the helm of American Baptist International Ministries. ANA ministry programs dedicated to cultivating the spiritual well-being and future of ANA congregations are surfacing at seminaries such as Fuller Theological Seminary, Talbot School of Theology, and Seattle Pacific University. ANAs are the dominant and majority ethnic group on many college and university campuses as well as in some mainline and evangelical seminaries. Books on ANA ministry and leadership written by ANA authors, both male and female, are steadily filling library shelves.[7] There are vibrant discussions about ministry in the ANA context on the internet. ANA preachers such as Eugene Cho, Ken Fong, David Gibbons, Soong-Chan Rah, Ken Shigematsu, and Ravi Zacharias are becoming household names in the dominant culture. However, we are saddened that there aren't even more touted ANA preachers' voices in North America, with ANA preachers headlining conferences being the norm rather than the exception. How we respond to the particular

---

7   See, for example, the growing body of literature from ANA authors such as: Eddie Byun, Peter Cha, Francis Chan, Simon Chan, Eugene Cho, James Choung, D. J. Chuang, Chris Chun, Sung Wook Chung, David Leong, David Gibbons, Young Lee Hertig, Albert Hsu, S. Steve Kang, Kathy Khang, Grace Ji-Sun Kim, Daniel Lee, Gregory Lee, Helen Lee, Paul C. H. Lim, Tom Lin, M. Sydney Park, Adrian Pei, Soong-Chan Rah, Ken Shigematsu, Benjamin Shin, Sarah Shin, Sheryl Takagi Silzer, Jonathan Tan, Siang-Yang Tan, John Teter, Al Tizon, Tim Tseng, Cindy Wu, Jenny Yang, Allen Yeh, Amos Yong, Ravi Zacharias, and others.

concerns facing ANA Christians will invite significant conversations
and require well-conceived strategies.

Besides being ANAs ourselves, we are grateful that God has called
and equipped us to write on this important topic. In addition to our
personal backgrounds mentioned above, Matthew wrote the first
PhD dissertation related to ANA preaching.[8] He served in pastoral
ministry as a youth pastor, college pastor, and senior pastor in Asian
congregations in Massachusetts and Colorado for nearly a decade.
He now serves as a professor of preaching and ministry and as the
director of the Haddon W. Robinson Center for Preaching at Gordon-
Conwell Theological Seminary in South Hamilton, Massachusetts.
He also is the author and editor of a number of books on preaching
and ministry.[9]

Daniel has served Chinese American and Canadian churches for
decades. He is a leading voice on the topic of ANA preaching and
has spoken at various ANA conferences and gatherings. Today, he
serves as a professor of Christian ministries at Tyndale University in
Toronto, Canada, and writes about multicultural issues in preaching
and ministry.[10]

---

8   See Matthew D. Kim, "Preaching to Second Generation Korean Americans:
Towards a Possible Selves Contextual Homiletic" (PhD dissertation, University of
Edinburgh, 2006); the published version is *Preaching to Second Generation Korean
Americans: Towards a Possible Selves Contextual Homiletic* (New York: Peter Lang, 2007).

9   Matthew D. Kim's books include: *7 Lessons for New Pastors: Your First Year in
Ministry* (Chalice, 2012), *Preaching with Cultural Intelligence: Understanding the People
Who Hear Our Sermons* (Baker Academic, 2017), *Homiletics and Hermeneutics: Four Views
on Preaching Today* (coeditor, Baker Academic, 2018), *A Little Book for New Preachers:
Why and How to Study Homiletics* (IVP Academic, 2020), *The Big Idea Companion to
Preaching and Teaching* (coeditor, Baker Academic, forthcoming), and *Preaching to
People in Pain* (tentative title, Baker Academic, forthcoming).

10   See, for example, Daniel L. Wong, "Preaching in a Multicultural World,"
Preaching: The Professional Journal for Preachers, 23:5 (March/April 2008): 12–16; "An
Intercultural Homiletic: Preaching Amidst Cultures," a paper presented at the 39th
Annual Meeting of the Academy of Homiletics, Memphis, Tennessee (2004): 308–16;
and "Multicultural Preaching and Its Implications for Pedagogy," a paper presented
at the 36th Annual Meeting of the Academy of Homiletics, St. Louis, Missouri (2001):
171–83. Other writing on preaching includes the "Homiletical Perspective" on John
3:22–30, 3:31–36, 4:1–6 in *Feasting on the Gospels, John, Vol. 1*, ed. Cynthia A. Jarvis and
E. Elizabeth Johnson (Louisville: Westminster John Knox, 2015).

You, as readers, also bring much to the conversation. We appreciate your continuous effort to preach faithful and relevant sermons for your people. The primary audience for this book is our fellow ANA pastors, elders, church leaders, parachurch workers, missionaries, and others who are interested in preaching to your own cultural and congregational contexts. But we hope this book will be relevant to others as well; perhaps you are one of many non-Asian pastors ministering and preaching to ANA listeners or you are a guest preacher in an ANA congregation. This book is also written with you in mind. As ANA preaching professors, we often receive questions from non-Asians about what it means to preach contextually for ANA congregants. Our hope in writing this book is that it will answer some of your theoretical and practical questions about your ANA hearers. A third audience is readers who are interested or involved in multicultural ministry and exploring ways that ethnicity affects preaching and ministry. A fourth readership may be first-generation Asian immigrant pastors seeking to join the conversation about how to preach more effectively to their children and their grandchildren. Finally, we have also written this book as an academic and practical resource for Bible college and seminary professors who are seeking a textbook for teaching on the topic of ANA ministry and preaching or multiethnic concerns.

THE PLAN OF THE BOOK

This book navigates five major conversation points. In the first four chapters, either Matthew or Daniel will take the lead and serve as the primary voice of the chapter. When Matthew uses the term "ANA," he is primarily speaking from an Asian American perspective, while Daniel employs it mainly in relation to Asian Canadians. At times, ANA will be used interchangeably for Americans or Canadians.

In chapter 1, Daniel describes the ANA experience and cultural narrative. Although persons of Asian descent have called America and Canada home for well over two centuries, ANAs remain "perpetual foreigners" and experience marginalization in the eyes of the dominant society. In chapter 2, Matthew addresses ANA hermeneutics and provides a short taxonomy of the common approaches by which ANAs interpret Scripture. He then shares a basic template for contextualized ANA hermeneutics. In chapter 3, Matthew continues with an overview of some of the major Asian and ANA theologies that have influenced ANA pastors and their doctrines, and he shows us a way to consider ANA theology going forward. In chapter 4, Daniel names common characteristics of today's ANA preachers and preaching. The final chapter, chapter 5, provides an opportunity for both authors to present a vision for the future of ANA homiletics. Each chapter articulates practical suggestions to help navigate the experiences, hermeneutics, theology, and preaching, respectively, in our both/and context. Questions for individual reflection and corporate discussion are provided at the conclusion of each chapter. Lastly, in the appendices, you will find a worksheet that will help you think through what it means to preach a sermon in an ANA context as well as two sample sermons we have preached to ANA audiences.

If you have ministered in an ANA context for a long time, preaching with ANAs in view might seem like a no-brainer. You may be saying, "Of course, Matthew and Daniel, that's what I do every Sunday!" However, may we submit to you that we might still be able to identify creative pathways to increase your contextualization for ANA listeners? You've probably heard the old Japanese proverb that says, "A nail that sticks out gets hammered down." Well, the good news is that we are not holding hammers in our hands, asking you to conform. Rather, we hope to give you a few more tools in your toolbox to preach the most effective sermons possible for your ANA congregants. Thank you for investing your time and energy into reading this book. We hope that by the end you will feel a little more equipped to put into practice some concrete homiletical skills to communicate effectively to ANAs and other hearers to the glory of our triune God.

Let the journey begin.

CHAPTER
ONE

Daniel L. Wong

THE ASIAN NORTH AMERICAN EXPERIENCE

Professor Sang Hyun Lee argued that first-generation immigrants' primary existential question is, "Why am I here?" ... First-generation ministry needs to offer theological resources that would help people to engage with this primary question. If so, I think second- and third-generation Asian [North] Americans wrestle with the question, "Who am I?" I think Asian [North] American preaching needs to address both of these questions from different theological angles, addressing both identity and calling (answering "why are we here?") in a meaningful way.

—Peter T. Cha, professor of church, culture, and society,
Trinity Evangelical Divinity School

"What are you?" "Where are you from?" "Where are you *really* from?" Questions like these bombard ANAs in their everyday life. Due to our appearance, we are presumed to have originated from an Asian country, have a particular Asian background, and speak an assumed "foreign" language. My most vivid memory of this kind of encounter stems from when I was outside my home in Markham, a suburb north of Toronto, stretching with my young children before we went for a jog in the neighborhood. A car filled with young people rolled down their windows and yelled like a chorus, "Welcome to Canada!" I instinctively started running after the car. I didn't want to pick a fight, but I did want to explain to them that my relatives have been in North America since the late 1800s. I am the same as them except I am a visible minority and I look like the many immigrants from Hong Kong and China who populate our area.

Such experiences affect my perception of self, how I interact with others, how I serve as a Christian, and even how I preach. Do you have similar experiences? In this chapter, I contend that the ANA experience is unique and different from both the white experience and the immigrant Asian experience. In particular, the history and journey of ANA listeners is marked by two competing narratives: that of the model minority and the perpetual foreigner. Due to the ongoing perpetuation of these narratives in North America, concrete reflection on these issues will result in making us more attentive and effective ANA preachers as we care for our ANA hearers who often struggle to make sense of who they are and how their identities impact their Christian life.

THE FORMATION OF IDENTITY

When we think of identity, we consider both our self-identity (what do I think of myself?) and an imposed identity (what do others think of me?). Our self-identity forms from early experiences with our nuclear family and extended family. Is there an environment of acceptance and love? When we go beyond these intimate spheres, a new world emerges of looks, judgments, and appellations. How we navigate this imposed identity is crucial for developing a healthy self-esteem.

Everyone struggles with personal identity. It is a part of growing up, and finding answers to our questions about identity has been called "the search for significance."[1] What complicates our identity

---

1   Robert S. McGee, *The Search for Significance: Seeing Your True Worth through God's Eyes*, revised and updated ed. (New York: Thomas Nelson, 2003).

as ANAs is that we are visible minorities. Consequently, we often struggle with accepting our appearance. The pressures that come with being visibly ethnic include Asian stereotypes, such as having excellent academic abilities. If we do not excel in school, we can experience self-loathing and shame. Theologian Grace Ji-Sun Kim states the added complexity of ANA identity formation this way: "Minorities are always asked to define themselves, or are identified with some form of adjective, while the white, European/American is never asked to define himself/herself. This actually allows the dominant, kyriarchical system to keep its presumptions of 'normativity,' while forcing those who do not fit that category to continually identify themselves."[2] She uses the term "kyriarchy" to mean anything having lordship or authority over another.

Identity is not a fixed feature of ourselves, like an arm. It is ever changing. Just as our physical selves are prone to grow and mature, so does our self-identity shift and expand over time. Gail Law developed the Dynamic Bi-Cultural Continuum Model to show that we fall somewhere on a spectrum between being more or less aligned with our traditional ethnic heritage.[3] Factors such as place of birth, cultural experience, type of family members and friends, schooling, type of church, where we live, and who we marry all affect movement along the Dynamic Bi-Cultural Continuum.

As an example, I often choose to identify myself based on the group I am among. At times, I have self-identified as an American-born Chinese, but since I have spent over half my life in Canada, I

2   Grace Ji-Sun Kim, "Do You Speak English? Racial Discrimination and Being the Other," *Grace Ji-Sun Kim ~ Loving Life* (blog), April 3, 2014, https://graceji sunkim.wordpress.com/2014/04/03/do-you-speak-english-racial-discrimination-and-being-the-other/. An extended version is found as "'Do You Speak English?' Racial Discrimination and Being the 'Perpetual Foreigner," in *Here I Am: Faith Stories of Korean American Clergywomen*, ed. Grace Ji-Sun Kim (Valley Forge, PA: Judson, 2015), 51–57.

3   Gail Law, "A Model for American Ethnic Chinese Churches," in *A Winning Combination: ABC/OBC Understanding the Cultural Tensions in Chinese Churches*, ed. Cecilia Yau (Petaluma, CA: Chinese Christian Mission, 1987), 131–41. The article first appeared in the December 1984 issue of *Theology, News & Notes*, published by Fuller Theological Seminary. This is an abridged version.

also consider myself a North American-born Chinese. For the purpose of this book, I am an Asian North American. We are hyphenated people, whether the hyphen actually appears or not. Fred Mok also shows this dynamic understanding of identity in relating his journey toward identifying himself as Asian American:

> I didn't realize I was Asian American until I moved to Atlanta in eighth grade. Before that, I was certain I was Chinese. In San Jose, I had lots of Chinese, Korean, and Japanese friends. We lived in the same affluent neighborhoods, were in the same accelerated classes, and had parents who worked for the same high-tech companies. We were plentiful. Despite the same immigrant emphasis on achievement, we were able to distinguish between Asian sub-groups. We didn't think about being Asian American until high school. At lunch time, we sat next to a low brick wall near the library. I later discovered my non-Asian classmates referred to the location as "The Great Wall."[4]

Like many ANAs, I struggled to accept who I was growing up. I often wished I could shed my yellow skin and just be Caucasian as my language and behavior indicated. When I became a Christian in high school, a Christian identity became a safe haven for me. I came to understand that there was a better place to root my identity and that is "in Christ" (2 Cor 5:17). This Christian identity surpassed race, ethnicity, and other factors. It connected me into the broader community and a family of believers, the body of Christ. Of course, identity in Christ does not obliterate one's skin color, cultural background,

---

4 Fred Mok, "The Otherness of Being Asian American," *Rant of the Exiles: Americanized Asians in the Immigrant Church* (blog), August 19, 2017, http://bread beforerice.blogspot.com/2017/08/the-otherness-of-being-asian-american.html.

gender, and accent. Even Jesus Christ, although portrayed in art in different ways, was Jewish.

The apostles Peter and Paul serve as helpful illustrations of Christian identity formation. Peter was thoroughly Jewish and needed a "conversion" just as much as a Christian from a gentile background.[5] We see Peter's struggle in Acts 10 in his openness to changing his perspective. I recall a Bible college professor saying that God was already moving Peter to openness as he stayed at the home of Simon the tanner (Acts 9:43). God prepared both Peter and Cornelius for a mutual encounter with the gospel.

The apostle Paul, while also Jewish, is an example of a bicultural, bilingual Christian. He was born in Tarsus, a largely Greek-speaking gentile city, so he was considered a Hellenistic Jewish person. He was embedded in his Jewish religion, leading him to become a rabbi. He was zealous in his misguided commitment to God, hotly pursuing and persecuting Christians. God stopped him dead in his tracks and effected his conversion (Acts 9, 22, and 27). Paul later came to understand who he was by the grace of God (1 Cor 15:10), and he could accept others based on Christ's acceptance of himself (Rom 15:7) because of his conversion experience. He did not forget his ethnic and religious upbringing. He could operate among many worlds by wisely working with others of various backgrounds.

A biblical understanding of identity facilitates the acceptance of self in all aspects of life. It provides hope and potential for every person found in Christ. In retrospect, I can see how God used my background to shape me into the person I am today. God used various experiences I had in Asian churches so that I could mentor and encourage others who serve in similar circumstances. Like many of us, there are certainly times when I question my identity and thus self-esteem, but I hasten back to Christ and find identity in him under his lordship.

---

5   Lesslie Newbigin underscored not only "the conversion of Cornelius, but also the conversion of Peter and the church" in *The Open Secret: Sketches for a Missionary Theology* (Grand Rapids: Eerdmans, 1981), 64.

ANA HISTORY AND IDENTITY

The identities of ANAs are tied to immigration history. I will not recount this history; there are many resources to explore the history of ANAs (especially abundant are those of Chinese and Korean ancestry in North America).[6] Suffice it to say, each time there has been a wave of immigration from Asian homelands, immigrants experience discrimination from mainstream residents and often from the government in the shape of various official exclusions, such as the Chinese Exclusion Act in the United States in 1882.

The first ones who leave their home country are called first-generation immigrants. Their children, depending on their age when coming to North America, are sometimes said to be 1.5-generation immigrants; they are bilingual and bicultural. Those born in North America are part of the second generation.[7] For the purposes of this book, we will include those who came to another country at a young age in the second generation, and the focus will be on this second generation and subsequent generations in North America.

First-generation immigrant parents often bemoan the fact that their children lose their language and culture, but this process is inevitable in immigrant communities. I have even heard Ken Fong comment to first-generation parents that it was their fault that their children lost their language and culture; after all, the parents decided to move to America. If they had not left their home country, their children would not have lost the language and culture. However,

---

6   See Iris Chang, *The Chinese in American: A Narrative History* (New York: Penguin, 2004); Peter S. Li, *Chinese in Canada*, 2nd ed. (Toronto: Oxford University Press, 2003); Grace J. Yoo, *Koreans in America: History, Identity, and Community*, rev. ed. (San Diego, CA: Cognella Academic Publishing, 2012); and Samuel Noh, Ann Kim, and Marianne Noh, *Korean Immigrants in Canada: Perspectives on Migration, Integration, and the Family* (Toronto: University of Toronto Press, 2012). The Chinese history in graphic form is *Escape to Gold Mountain: A Graphic History of the Chinese in North America* by David H. T. Wong (Vancouver: Arsenal Pulp, 2012).

7   A substantial amount of research has been done on second-generation Americans with a particular focus on Asian Americans and Hispanics; Pew Social Trends, February 7, 2013, http://www.pewsocialtrends.org/2013/02/07/second-generation-americans/.

these days, Western influences are hard to resist even in the home culture due to the ubiquitous internet. Fong uses the analogy of fish to describe the cultural transformation among later generations. He calls this the "inevitable flow of generations."[8] Asian immigrants are freshwater fish like bass. The second generation are more like salmon, which swim downstream to salt water as they mature. They are adaptable fish, going between culture and languages. The third generation are acculturated cod who speak only English. They are saltwater fish who are at home in the new environment.

It seems that the further ANAs get away from the immigrant experience, the more curious they are about their family history and identity. While the second generation can be at odds with their first-generation parents, third-generation ANAs like me often seek out their roots. Maybe they take a genetic test or explore the oral history of their family. I found that my paternal grandfather immigrated to the United States and settled in San Francisco. No doubt he came through Angel Island, the entry point for the Pacific at that time. All I know about him is that he was a "paper son," going under the assumed name of Wong, pretending to be the son of another family to get into the States. My middle name is Lee, which was his real last name. I wonder how old he was when he arrived. What did he do subsequently? Was his wedding an arranged one? I know more about my mother's side. My great-grandmother was born in the Monterey Bay area. Her parents and others traveled from the Canton province of China by small ships to arrive on the California coast, making their livelihood by fishing.

Being born in America and then living in Canada for half of my life, I have noticed there are some key differences between Asian Americans and Asian Canadians. One is the context of race in each country. The United States is viewed racially as black and white, with

---

8   Ken Uyeda Fong, *Pursuing the Pearl: A Comprehensive Resource for Multi-Asian Ministry* (Valley Forge, PA: Judson, 1999), 19–23.

other groups filling in the middle.[9] Canada is viewed as a multi-cultural country, affirming cultural diversity. Another difference between the countries is that Canada has a more accepting political attitude toward receiving immigrants than the United States. And third, from its strong British connection, Canada has adopted the British way of accepting multiculturalism into its culturally diverse empire. These differences weigh heavily on ANAs' self-identity and imposed identity. I find esteem issues more rampant in the United States, where the pressure to assimilate continues. This comes from the antiquated understanding of the United States as a melting pot, calling to mind a cartoonish image of a pot with people being dumped in as the ingredients.[10]

While Canada can feel more inclusive, this does not mean that there are not pockets of racism and discrimination, especially in times of terrorism and our post-9/11 world. Having a parliamentary system also affects the day-to-day life of Canadians and the political climate. Canada is more akin to European countries with their post-Christian realities. Since most Asians live in major cities in Canada, ethnic ingredients, food, and restaurants are readily available. One Asian Canadian commented, "I think the Asian Canadian experience depends on how deeply one assimilates Canadian culture, fluency and command of languages, and general mindset."[11] While Asian Canadians can assimilate to a degree, there is still naturally a tension. Skin color is not invisible, nor does it fully blend in with others.

---

9   David A. Anderson calls the blacks and whites "bookends" for "middle books" of other races and ethnic groups in *Multicultural Ministry: Finding Your Church's Unique Rhythm* (Grand Rapids: Zondervan, 2004), 19.

10   See "Schoolhouse Rock—The Great American Melting Pot," from 1977, https://www.youtube.com/watch?v=5ZQl6XBo64M.

11   Michael Chang, "What Is It like Being Asian Canadian?," Quora (website), July 28, 2016, https://www.quora.com/What-is-it-like-being-an-Asian-Canadian.

PARENTAL EXPECTATIONS

A perennial issue experienced by ANAs in the second generation and beyond is the expectation from parents to achieve. This is a major complaint of ANA children, youth, and young adults that gave rise to Amy Chua's image of the "tiger mom."[12] The problem arises from well-meaning parents who sacrificed a career and life in their home country to immigrate to North America for the sake of giving their children a better life. Children are regularly reminded of this fact.

A central teaching in Scripture that is seized on in Asian culture is honoring your parents. The prevalence of this teaching led me to write my master of theology thesis on "An Exegetical and Theological Study of the Fifth Commandment."[13] In the Old Testament economy, honoring parents is about maintaining the continuity of the covenant. In the New Testament, Jesus affirmed the fifth commandment and set the example of honoring parents. He provided for the care of his mother after his crucifixion. One can be considered worse than an unbeliever if one does not care for an aging parent (1 Tim 5:8). This care includes financial compensation toward one's parents and grandparents.

While honoring parents is a good cultural and theological practice, there needs to be some parsing. It does not mean to obey parents even to the disobedience of God. There ought to be a correlation between honoring parents and honoring God. Honoring is not equivalent to obeying. The child must decide when following Christ may be at odds with obeying parents. Disobedience to parents can still be honoring them when it is done in a communicative and loving way.

The way a person views God is often built on the relationship with parents, particularly with one's father. If the father is seen as strict and demanding, this often results in viewing God the same

---

12   Amy Chua, *The Battle Hymn of the Tiger Mom* (New York: Penguin, 2011). To provide a Christian answer to combat the "tiger mom" syndrome, Helen Lee wrote *Missional Mom: Living with Purpose at Home & in the World* (Chicago: Moody, 2011).

13   Daniel L. Wong, "An Exegetical and Theological Study of the Fifth Commandment" (ThM thesis, Dallas Theological Seminary, May 1981).

way, especially when addressing God as heavenly Father. (We develop "God as Father" as a preaching topic in chapter 5.) There are great expectations on firstborn sons and great stigma for wayward ones. Even if the son is not technically the firstborn because he has older sisters, the position of firstborn son is significant. The image of the elder brother in the parable of the prodigal son may provide some parallels.

Paul Tokunaga lays out specific expectations that are common among ANA families: (1) to get a good education, (2) to remain children until they marry, (3) to marry the right person, which means marrying within one's ethnicity, and (4) to stay within one's community, which often means staying within one's ethnic circles, including the ethnic church.[14] Most ANAs experience these to varying degrees. Next, I will explore common expectations surrounding language, education, career, marriage, and children.

Language

Second-generation ANAs have to navigate ethnic language fluency. Some immigrant parents speak to their children exclusively in their mother tongue. Some parents diligently send their children to a language school that is based on writing and memorizing rather than oral conversation. Often these language schools are housed in churches. I often wonder whether there is a good or bad taste in the mouths of these children when they reflect on their experience at church. In Korean churches, the Sunday school through the primary years is frequently in Korean. In Chinese churches, once the child goes to school, English is used in Sunday school.

As a third-generation Chinese American, I only began language school in college where I started to study Mandarin Chinese. I also took some Cantonese classes for adults. I later learned a lot

---

14   Paul Tokunaga, "Pressure, Perfectionism & Performance," in *Following Jesus without Dishonoring Your Parents,* by Jeanette Yep, Peter Cha, Susan Cho, Van Riesen, Greg Jao, and Paul Tokunaga (Downers Grove, IL: InterVarsity, 1998), 22–26.

of Cantonese through osmosis by serving in Cantonese-speaking churches in Toronto. My wife is from Taiwan and speaks primarily Mandarin Chinese. If you want to learn a language, fall in love with someone who speaks that language. My Mandarin has definitely improved. While my children were not sent to Chinese school in their younger years, both elected to learn more Mandarin in high school and beyond. My son spent a year and a quarter in Taiwan teaching English. He not only picked up Mandarin, the national language of Taiwan but also some Taiwanese, a Chinese dialect spoken by a majority of residents.

Language capabilities have been an advantage to me in life and in ministry. While many children, like me, will one day be grateful for language study, there is a wide language gap between children and their parents and grandparents. Both sides need to make the effort to communicate and understand each other.

Education

As mentioned in the preface, Matthew's parents strategically moved to a location that had a good school district for their children. In some ANA families, this move may take place even before the children are born. How better to get a good start than to get a good education? Parents may even move to a smaller residence just to be in the right school district. To make sure their students can compete with others, the parents may enroll them in after-school and weekend courses to enhance math, science, English, and other skills. In Canada, there is no standardized test like the SAT for university or college entrance. The key factor for admissions is grade point average, producing higher expectations for student grades.

ANA parents want their children to get into the right school and the right field of study. The "right" field is a professional one, such as a medical doctor (even specialist), dentist, engineer, accountant, or lawyer. Those careers that are non-professional or artistic are often frowned upon. Having a son or daughter go to an Ivy League school provides bragging rights to the parents' family and friends. Even life savings are spent and houses mortgaged to facilitate this education.

This means the young person who experiences a call to ministry often finds resistance. Even if the parents are Christians, the child may be dissuaded from proceeding in that direction. It is ironic that even some parents who dedicate their children to the Lord at a young age will balk if the Lord wants to call the child in a direction contrary to the parents' wishes. I know one young person who did not consider ministry an option for fear of being disowned by his parents. How could you honor your parents by throwing away a hard-earned education by going into ministry? That is only for people who are unable to make it in other fields. It is even worse to become a missionary or a campus ministry worker, who has to raise funds. Why depend on other people? Why waste your education? Why bother?

Career

Closely related to education is one's choice of career. As mentioned above, parents expect that their children will go into professional careers that are high paying and bring financial stability. Some young ANAs enter a professional career for a few years in an attempt to respect their parents in line with filial piety before attempting something that they are actually passionate about. Some have done this before fulfilling a ministry calling.

I try to encourage ANA youth to find how God has wired them. For myself, it definitely was not in math and science. If I didn't have a calling for ministry, it would have been in social work, as I enjoy helping people. In contrast to many first-generation parents, my second-generation parents did not push me into a particular career. They offered to pay for two years of college for wherever I wanted to go, and they encouraged me to study two years at a junior college so I could later receive a BA degree at Moody Bible Institute. Otherwise, I would have only earned a certificate.

There has been a lot of pain and tears shed over the contrasting expectations between North-American-born children and their immigrant parents in the area of career. Jeanette Yep recounts her painful journey to healing with her parents after pursuing her education and ministry calling. She attributes her ability to step into this career path to friends who journeyed with her, those within her extended family, and the resource of the Holy Spirit to be able to forgive and heal painful memories.[15]

A recent development is that we are now seeing more ANAs in the entertainment industry. *Crazy Rich Asians* was a blockbuster with a primarily Asian cast. American-born Constance Wu (*Fresh Off the Boat*) and Ken Jeong (*Dr. Ken* and movies) play key roles in the film. It is the first big Hollywood movie with a primarily Asian cast since *The Joy Luck Club* (1993). Fitting the pattern I noted above, Jeong practiced as an internal medicine specialist before shifting to acting full-time. D. K. Jeong, Ken's father, a retired economics professor, once said, "I promised him that if he got into medical school, I would give him the opportunity to develop his hobby and go anywhere in the world to develop his hobby."[16] Ken did not leave medicine until his acting career took off.

Simu Liu, who plays a Korean son in the Canadian television comedy *Kim's Convenience,* was born in Harbin, China, and immigrated to Canada with his parents at age five. He decided to become an actor after he was laid off from his accounting job.[17] It was painful to inform his parents, but he was able to pursue his personal acting

15   Jeanette Yep, "Your Parents Love You, My Parents Love Me," in *Following Jesus without Dishonoring Your Parents.*

16   Jen Chaney, "Ken Jeong: From Doctor to Comedic Actor, with a 'Hangover' in Between," *Washington Post,* May 20, 2011, https://www.washingtonpost.com/entertainment/movies/ken-jeong-from-doctor-to-comedic-actor-with-a-hangover-in-between/2011/05/17/AFbRvt7G_story.html.

17   Tracy G. Lee, "'Kim's Convenience' Actor Simu Liu on being an Accountant, His Big Break, and 'Crazy Rich Asians' Momentum," *NBC News,* August 31, 2018, https://www.nbcnews.com/news/asian-america/kim-s-convenience-actor-simu-liu-being-accountant-his-big-n904911. A written letter to Liu's parents, "A Chinese Canadian to His Parents: Privately I Yearned for Your Love," reveals his inner

interest. He will be the first Asian Marvel superhero, Shang-Chi, in an upcoming movie. Ins Choi, the creator of *Kim's Convenience,* comes from a line of pastors. His grandfather wanted him to follow the family tradition. Choi went for a year to Tyndale University (where I teach) when it was called Ontario Bible College and took a course in drama. Later he graduated from York University in drama. While he didn't go into ministry, his novel and subsequent stage play with the same name is based on the biblical story of the prodigal son.

Another area that has seen an increase in ANA involvement is sports. Michael Chang is one example of a model athlete who is also a Christian. At age seventeen, he won the French Open tennis tournament, the youngest to do so at the time. His quiet demeanor and tenacity won the hearts of ANAs and others. When asked for an autograph, he would write the acronym PTL (for "Praise the Lord"). Jeremy Lin is another Christian ANA role model. He played basketball for Harvard before finding his way to the NBA. He has connections with InterVarsity Christian Fellowship and publicly speaks and posts about his Christian faith. His Twitter bio states, "To know Him is to want to know Him more."[18] The height of his career with the New York Knicks in 2012 became known as "Linsanity" due to his clutch play. Asian Americans and Asian immigrants would flood the games. When the Knicks played the Toronto Raptors, Asian Canadian fans would cheer for him more than their home team. He often speaks of the numerous setbacks he has faced with injuries and the discrimination he has faced on and off the court. As of this writing, his career in the NBA has waned; he currently plays in China for the Beijing Ducks.

---

feelings: https://www.macleans.ca/opinion/a-chinese-canadian-to-his-parents-privately-i-yearned-for-your-love. I heard him recount his story and field questions at the Markham Village Branch, Markham Public Library, May 12, 2018.

18   Jeremy Lin, https://twitter.com/JLin7.

Marriage

Choosing a spouse reflects one's self-identity and the people one wants to relate to in society. First-generation Asian parents in North America tend to prefer for their children to marry a person of their own ethnic background, ideally who speaks the same language and dialect as the parents. Further, dating should only take place post-university, when one has an established career. If a child crosses ethnic lines, many Asian parents quickly disapprove. There are some who marry ANAs of a different generation, like a third-generation person with a first-generation. My wife, for example, never ventured off the island of Taiwan until we were married.

Of course, marrying outside of one's ethnic background ("out-marriage") occurs as well. Conflicts can increase when this happens, even if a second-generation Korean marries a second-generation Chinese. Anecdotally, out-marriage is more common between Caucasian men and Asian women, whether first or subsequent generations. It is less common for an Asian man to marry a Caucasian woman, but it does happen; my son married a Scottish/Dutch woman who has blue eyes and blond hair. She spent over a year in China teaching English, gaining conversational ability in Mandarin. Fred Mok highlights some of the stereotypes of Asian women and men when it comes to marriage: "In Western culture, Asian women are fetishized. They're so sexy, petite, mysterious, docile, and submissive. That stereotype has the opposite effect on the sexual attractiveness of Asian men, who are hyper-feminized, emasculated, and compared against a toxic Western ideal of masculinity, especially when it comes to physical appearance."[19] Matthew further discusses these stereotypes in chapter 3.

---

19   Fred Mok, "Do Asian American Women Have More Courage than Men?," *Rant of the Exiles: Americanized Asians in the Immigrant Church* (blog), July 13, 2018, http://breadbeforerice.blogspot.com/2018/07/do-asian-american-women-have-more.html.

Children and Parents

First-generation Asian parents expect their children to bear children. Once their child is married, the pressure is on for the couple to have a child. That is, of course, easier said than done. In the Bible, Sarah, Hannah, and Elizabeth all required a miracle for them to have a child, and issues of infertility are common today as well. If God provides a child, particularly firstborn sons have a cultural expectation of carrying on the family line and taking care of aging parents.

For some first-generation parents, there is still a stigma attached to adoption, but this seems to be less common in the second generation and later. A lot of adjustment needs to be made by all of the family involved. Nevertheless, it is a blessing to be involved in adoption. My son and daughter-in-law experienced this privilege when they adopted a three-year-old boy from China in November 2017. Ken Fong and his wife adopted Janessa, an American-born Chinese, and he developed the biblical narrative connecting to adoption in his book *Secure in God's Embrace.*[20]

It is an unfortunate part of ANA identity that many ANAs feel guilt and shame if they do not live up to the expectations of their parents and themselves. Parents certainly mean well to encourage their children to do well in life, especially to facilitate financial success. However, Christian parents may find themselves at odds with God's desire for their children. Not all children will go to an Ivy League school and have a professional career. Not all will marry within their own ethnicity. Not all will be able to produce children, particularly a male heir.

DJ Chuang has an excellent podcast, *Erasing Shame,* which explores issues related to shame in the ANA context.[21] Issues of guilt and shame are deeply embedded in the culture of immigrant families. These issues affect self-esteem and contribute to addictive behavior.

---

20   Ken Fong, *Secure in God's Embrace: Living as the Father's Adopted Child* (Downers Grove, IL: InterVarsity, 2006).

21   See DJ Chuang, *Erasing Shame,* http://erasingshame.com.

A counseling perspective is developed by Sam Louie in his article, "Asian Shame and Honor."[22] Drug use and suicide are also results of living under the burden of a shame-based culture. Matthew expands more on this theme in chapter 2, and we offer suggestions for preaching on shame and pain in chapter 5.

CHURCH IDENTITY

In addition to cultural history and expectations from parents, church is often a major factor in the identity of many second-generation ANAs. Many of us have had formative experiences in immigrant churches. The two largest types of Asian immigrant churches in North America are the Korean and the Chinese. In 2013, there were 4,233 Korean churches in the United States (1,358 in California alone) and 476 in Canada.[23] There were an estimated 1,679 Chinese churches in the United States in 2014.[24] There were 496 Chinese churches in Canada in 2018.[25] Many of these churches have English worship services or youth worship services. In many ways, second-generation and beyond ANAs feel like a visible minority in the society and also an invisible minority in the church. I call this a double marginality. If a person is not fluent in the immigrant church's primary language, then that person is often excluded from consideration for the main leadership of the church.

The Silent Exodus

Many immigrant Asian families have developed their Christian faith or have become Christians. They raise their children in the church,

---

22   Sam Louie, "Asian Shame and Honor," *Psychology Today,* June 29, 2014, https://www.psychologytoday.com/ca/blog/minority-report/201406/asian-shame-and-honor. See his "5 Facts about Asian-American Christian Shame," *Psychology Today,* 23 September 2015, https://www.psychologytoday.com/ca/blog/minority-report/201509/5-facts-about-asian-american-christian-shame.

23   DJ Chuang, "Number of Korean Churches in the USA and Canada," *@djchuang* (blog), June 2, 2014, https://djchuang.com/2014/number-korean-churches-usa.

24   DJ Chuang, "How Many Chinese Churches Are in the USA?," *@djchuang* (blog), July 19, 2014, https://djchuang.com/2014/many-chinese-churches-usa.

25   GO International Canada, November 2018 newsletter (in Chinese).

but the children do not always adopt the faith for themselves. This is true of any child raised in the church. Particularly in the ANA church setting, the departure of children from the church is referred to as "the silent exodus." It is silent in that it is "happening almost unnoticed," and it is an exodus "because the size of the departure [is] massive and the numbers staggering.'"[26]

In 1997, Minho Song delineated a number of reasons for the silent exodus from Korean churches.[27] The first was too much emphasis on Korean ethnicity. This came from an obligation to meet the needs of first-generation Koreans. A second reason was the power of the postmodern culture that could erode the spiritual life of second-generation Koreans. The third was structural limitations. If the church is run by the first generation, who speaks Korean, the second generation finds it difficult to get involved in the main leadership of the church without fluency in Korean. The fourth reason was an unclear future of the Korean immigrant church. These churches tend to be insular and not open to reaching beyond their own people. The fifth was church splits and other negative experiences. These experiences haven't made church a very appealing place for long-term commitment and involvement. Enoch Wong has noted that the silent exodus also occurs among Chinese Christians, but it's not as pronounced as among Koreans.[28]

---

26   Rebecca Y. Kim, "Made in the U.S.A.: Second Generation Korean American Campus Evangelicals," in *Asian American Youth: Culture, Identity, and Ethnicity*, ed. Jennifer Lee and Min Zhou (New York: Routledge, 2004), 237–38.

27   Minho Song, "Constructing a Local Theology for the Second Generation Korean Ministry," *Urban Mission* 15:2 (Dec 1997): 23–24.

Helen Lee alerted the broader Christian community to this phenomenon in "Silent Exodus: Can the East Asian Church in America Reverse the Flight of Its Next Generation?," *Christianity Today* (August 12, 1996), 50–53.

28   Enoch Kin On Wong, "'How Am I Going to Grow Up?' An Exploration of Congregational Transition Among Second-Generation Chinese Canadian Evangelicals and Servant-Leadership" (PhD dissertation, Gonzaga University, 2015), 118. See also Matthew Richard Sheldon Todd, *English Ministry Crisis in Chinese Canadian Churches: Towards the Retention of English-Speaking Adults from Chinese Canadian Church through Associated Parallel Independent English Congregational Models* (Eugene, OR: Wipf & Stock, 2015); and *Developing a Transformational English Ministry in Chinese Churches* (Victoria, BC: FriesenPress, 2016).

Some suggestions for stemming the tide of the silent exodus include changing the church structure so that it is less hierarchical and changing the church's mission so that it expands beyond immigrant ministry only.[29] Also, a commitment to radical discipleship by the second generation is crucial. Moreover, they need to see this modeled by church leaders and parents. It may be helpful to shift to a church model of autonomy where the second generation has decision-making power and takes ownership over leadership development. Minho Song's church, for example, has an English congregation called "Church on a Hill" led by an American-born, second-generation Korean pastor under the shadow of a Korean church. However, conflicts and challenges will likely arise between language congregations in a church housed within the ethnic immigrant church.

While it is not part of the silent exodus, there is also the phenomenon of leaving an ethnic church to go to white American or Canadian churches. Often, however, ANA persons do not get involved to the extent that they would in an ethnic church. Ideally, English-speaking churches would aim to be more multiracial, multiethnic, and multicultural to represent the diverse body of Christ.

The Role of Women

Another particular challenge among ANA churches is the role of women. According to David Ng, "The Confucian and Asian heritage has, over the years, evolved into a social system that has not valued women."[30] According to this Confucian heritage, the man is placed over the woman in a proposed harmonious society. This has often been replicated in the church. Men play the primary roles and women play supportive ones in church and in the family. I recognize there are ongoing debates about the theological perspective of the role of

---

29   From Minho Song, "Constructing a Local Theology," 7–10.

30   David Ng, "Varieties of Congregations for Varieties of People" in *People on the Way: Asian North Americans Discovering Christ, Culture, and Community*, ed. David Ng (Valley Forge, PA: Judson, 1996), 293.

women in ministry.[31] In many places a woman may serve, but not in ordained ministry or in a senior role. In other denominations, that opportunity exists. However, even where the possibility is available, communities of believers are slow to accept this because of their patriarchal history. It is the cultural overtones, not the theology, that make it difficult for women to enter leadership positions. Whatever theological perspective one takes, women need to be affirmed and valued in society and in the church.

Some women have served extensively and effectively in parachurch organizations or at their university. They may have served in multiethnic ministries such as InterVarsity Christian Fellowship and attended the Urbana triennial mission convention and experienced a world beyond their own ethnic group. But when reentering the ANA church, they may be frustrated that opportunities for ministry are limited and often suppressed. This can prevent a return to the ethnic church in favor of other churches.

MISTAKEN IDENTITY

In addition to parental and church expectations as shapers of ANA identity, we must also speak of mistaken perceptions of ANAs that at times result in outright racism and discrimination. Etched in the minds and hearts of many Asian Americans is the tragic story of Vincent Chin.[32] In 1982, Chin had his bachelor party at a club in Detroit. He was Chinese American, but local autoworkers assumed that he was Japanese and was taking jobs away from American

---

31 Matthew has written a cogent piece in favor of gender equality with particular consideration of the Korean American church entitled "Korean America—Challenging the Patriarchal Ethos: Gender Equality in the Korean American Church," in *Global Voices on Biblical Equality: Women and Men Ministering Together in the Church*, ed. Aida Besançon Spencer, William David Spencer, and Mimi Haddad (Eugene, OR: Wipf & Stock, 2008), 52–69.

32 Frances Kai-Hwa Wang, "Who Is Vincent Chin? The History and Relevance of a 1982 Killing," *NBC News*, June 15, 2017, https://www.nbcnews.com/news/asian-america/who-vincent-chin-history-relevance-1982-killing-n771291.

workers. He was beaten with a baseball bat and subsequently succumbed to his injuries. Today, we would call this a hate crime, and it ended up being one of the catalysts of the Asian American civil rights movement.

As a visible minority in North America, ANAs experience discrimination and racism regularly. One poll of Asian Americans that included US-born Asian Americans and immigrants showed the following regarding personal experiences of discrimination:

> Overall, Asian Americans report numerous personal experiences of discrimination, across many areas of life. In the context of institutional forms of discrimination, a quarter or more of Asian Americans say they have been personally discriminated against because they are Asian when applying for jobs (27%), when being paid equally or considered for promotions (25%), and when trying to rent or buy housing (25%). In the context of individual forms of discrimination, about a third of Asian Americans say they have personally experienced racial or ethnic slurs (32%) and people making negative assumptions or insensitive or offensive comments about their race or ethnicity (35%). Non-immigrant Asian Americans are significantly more likely than their immigrant counterparts to report multiple forms of individual discrimination, including threats or non-sexual harassment, sexual harassment, and violence. Immigrants, however, are more likely to report experiencing discrimination when seeking healthcare.[33]

---

33 "Discrimination in America: Experiences and Views of Asian Americans," November 2017, https://www.npr.org/assets/news/2017/12/discriminationpoll-asian-americans.pdf.

One Korean American, reporting on a hazing incident of an American-born Chinese at an Asian American fraternity, asserted, "Discrimination is what ties Asian Americans together."[34]

Who among us as ANAs has not experienced mistaken identity? Even when it does not extend to outright discrimination and racism, we are mistaken for another ethnic origin. We are born in the United States or Canada, but it is assumed that we are from overseas. Since ANAs are visible minorities, we continually run into one or both of two common mistaken identities: that of the model minority and the perpetual foreigner.

Model Minority

The stereotype of the "model minority" arose in the mid-1960s at the height of the civil rights and ethnic consciousness movements, but before the rising waves of immigration and refugee influx from Asia.[35] According to this stereotype, others view Asians as intelligent, hardworking, and law-abiding. Often, distinct Asian groups are homogenized into one, and it is assumed that there are no cultural or socioeconomic disparities between them. This stereotype is primarily associated with the United States and draws on perceived distinctions between Asians and African Americans. Fred Mok notes, "In the US, the model minority stereotype is a stunted privilege but a privilege nonetheless. We hear about it. We benefit from it. We reinforce it."[36]

An important critique of the model minority stereotype is that it excludes those that are not a part of it. It pits ethnic groups against each other. It also negates those who don't fit the stereotype. Those from socioeconomic classes who don't fit the stereotype are excluded.

---

34   Jay Caspian Kang, "What a Fraternity Hazing Death Revealed about the Painful Search for an Asian-American Identity," *New York Times,* August 9, 2017, https://www.nytimes.com/2017/08/09/magazine/what-a-fraternity-hazing-death-revealed-about-the-painful-search-for-an-asian-american-identity.html.

35   Zhou and Lee, *Asian American Youth,* 18.

36   Fred Mok, "The Otherness of Being Asian American."

Yet there are also positive aspects of being considered a model minority. Others view ANAs in a positive light, and we don't face as much discrimination as other groups do. Greg Jao of InterVarsity pointed out how the gospel could interact with this stereotype when Tom Lin became president of InterVarsity Christian Fellowship/ USA in 2016: "Tom's story reflects the way the gospel intersects the 'model minority' narrative. He's an academic all-star who has submitted to Jesus' claims to his talent and future. He's wrestled with obtaining parental approval. He's broken through the bamboo ceiling that often confronts Asian Americans in the corporate world which always question our credentials."[37] Jao himself is another example of the intersection of the gospel and the model minority narrative. He serves as Director of External Relations for InterVarsity Christian Fellowship/USA. Before his ministry with InterVarsity, Jao was an attorney in Chicago.

Perpetual Foreigner

The perpetual foreigner stereotype means that ANAs are seen as non-Americans or non-Canadians. Based on our appearance, people assume that we don't speak English or that we are from overseas. Theologian Grace Ji-Sun Kim wrote about her experience of going in and out of a hospital in an area where she lives where English is predominantly spoken. The first thing the doctor asked was, "Do you speak English?" After they had been speaking for about five minutes, a nurse suddenly asked her, "Is English your preferred language?" Both of these questions grate upon one who may look "foreign" but is, in fact, an English speaker without a foreign accent.

Being seen as a perpetual foreigner is part of the struggle ANAs are faced with throughout their lives. One well-known example of the perpetual foreigner stereotype is the internment of the Japanese

---

37 Kate Shellnutt, "InterVarsity Names a Historic New President," *Christianity Today,* May 16, 2016, https://www.christianitytoday.com/ct/2016/may-web-only/ intervarsity-names-historic-new-president.html.

during World War II, in which many were incarcerated who were American citizens. My mother recalls many Chinese in San Francisco at the time wearing badges stating that they were not Japanese. I recall one time when a missionary came to address our class at Moody Bible Institute. He made a reference to someone who lived overseas, "like my brother over there." I looked around. He was referring to me. At that point, I had never been overseas or even visited a "foreign" country like Mexico or Canada.

A cashier at a grocery store may hold up her hand with five fingers extended and say "five dollars" in slow and clear English. Or someone may speak to you first in Mandarin Chinese or Cantonese, assuming that you understand. Even many fellow Asians can't tell the difference between different groups and whether someone speaks English as their first language.[38] During one of our conversations, Michael Soon Lee provided an excellent question to ask when curious about someone's ethnic or racial background: "Where are your ancestors from?"[39] Anyone can be asked this open-ended question. It does not assume a person's foreignness or origins.

American-born Asian Michael Luo summed up the thoughts of many ANAs when he wrote an open letter in response to a woman who yelled "Go back to China!" at him: "Maybe you don't know this, but the insults you hurled at my family get to the heart of the Asian-American experience. It's this persistent sense of otherness that a lot of us struggle with every day. That no matter what we do, how successful we are, what friends we make, we don't belong. We're foreign. We're not American."[40]

---

38   Take this test to guess if a person is Chinese, Japanese, or Korean based on appearance: "How to Tell Chinese, Korean and Japanese Apart," Off the Great Wall, March 10, 2015, https://www.youtube.com/watch?v=VLiYqMwKpK8.

39   See this humorous clip with a person whose grandparents are from England asking an ANA, "Where are you from?," YouTube, May 31, 2013, https://www.youtube.com/watch?v=crAv5ttax2l.

40   "An Open Letter to the Woman Who Told My Family to Go Back to China," *New York Times,* October 9, 2016, https://www.nytimes.com/2016/10/10/nyregion/to-the-woman-who-told-my-family-to-go-back-to-china.html.

ANAs internalize experiences of racism and discrimination because we are often lumped together with immigrants. We want to be viewed as American or Canadian without an asterisk. We want members of the dominant culture to assume that we're North American and not a recent immigrant based on what we look like on the outside. As a result of this feeling of otherness, ANAs can live with a chip on our shoulder. We don't fit neatly anywhere in society— not with immigrants and not with whites. We should be willing to confront stereotypes such as the model minority and the perpetual foreigner. When done with a loving spirit, these miscues can become a touchstone of conversation with those within and outside of ANA communities. They become catalysts for us to become missional, spreading our faith through our own cultural lenses.

CONCLUSION

Minho Song asserts, "The formation of a healthy ethnic identity is one of the greatest tasks facing [second-generation] Koreans today."[41] We can add other ANAs to his assertion as well. This issue of ANA identity cannot be ignored. As marginalized people, our sense of our own in-betweenness often negatively affects how we live as Christians. For this reason, sermons in an ANA context cannot remain generic and culture free. We must speak to the heart of the ANA experience. That is what the rest of the book is about.

We will revisit the subject of identity later in the book, especially when Matthew develops "Identity and the Image of God" in chapter 3. My sample sermon in appendix 2 centers on the theme of identity as well. A healthy self-identity and understanding of self creates a solid foundation for preachers and preaching in the ANA context.

The first step in preaching well in an ANA context is to approach the Scripture through ANA eyes, to make sure we are addressing

---

41　Minho Song, "Patterns of Religious Participation among the Second-Generation Koreans in Toronto: Toward the Analysis and Prevention of 'The Silent Exodus'" (PhD dissertation, Trinity Evangelical Divinity School, 1999), 19.

questions and concerns brought about by the ANA experience. This leads us to our major question addressed in the next chapter: How should ANAs interpret the Bible?

QUESTIONS FOR REFLECTION
AND DISCUSSION

1. How do you describe yourself racially and ethnically?
2. How do others describe/call you?
3. What experiences have you had of being stereotyped?
4. How has Christianity shaped your identity?
5. Who are your ANA role models?
6. How might you help others accept their ANA identity?

CHAPTER
TWO

Matthew D. Kim

ASIAN NORTH AMERICAN HERMENEUTICS

I urge every generation of Asian preachers to let God be their first and only standard of effectiveness. Be expositors of God's word. Bridge the gap between the treasures in Scripture and how valuable they are for today's context. Mine those truths tenaciously. Prepare a feast for your listeners by building their appetite and their expectation to hear from God. Live by the power of the Spirit to consistently deliver the good news in a winsome, logical, and timely fashion that transforms lives for eternity.

—Bruce W. Fong, dean and professor of preaching,
Dallas Theological Seminary, Houston campus

When we read the Bible, we don't simply read its contents. Rather, every time we read Scripture we become "a hermeneut" or an interpreter.[1] When I read the Bible with my children, I encourage them to ask any and all questions that they have because there is so much in Scripture that is unfamiliar to them. They ask me who a Samaritan was or why the Pharisees tried to hurt Jesus. My

---

1   Raymond Bailey, "Hermeneutics: A Necessary Art," introduction in *Hermeneutics for Preaching: Approaches to Contemporary Interpretations of Scripture*, ed. Raymond Bailey (Nashville: Broadman, 1992), 7.

sons are not simply readers of the Bible who attempt to phonetically sound out words correctly; they are young interpreters.[2] Similarly, while a "plain reading" of the text is possible, the struggle for preachers is that we do not interpret in isolation, nor are we interpreting biblical cultures that are necessarily familiar to us. William Klein, Craig Blomberg, and Robert Hubbard Jr. explain: "On the pages of the Bible we encounter customs, beliefs, and practices that make little sense to us."[3] Stated differently, the Bible contains foreign languages written by foreign authors from foreign cultures to foreign readers for foreign times.[4] The very foreignness of Scripture presents peculiar obstacles for twenty-first-century preachers, and that, of course, includes ANA expositors.

Hermeneutics is a complicated endeavor for any interpreter, but it can be even more so for those ANA interpreters who remain liminal or culturally in limbo—identifying with aspects of American/Canadian culture as well as Asian cultures. If you are an ANA person, do you interpret the Bible exactly like white North Americans? If you are an ANA preacher, do you exposit Scripture exactly like your white/Euro-American preaching colleagues? Have you ever wondered if your Asian-ness factors into the hermeneutical process? We seldom talk about this exegetical nuance in churches and in seminaries. As such, "Asian [North] American biblical interpretation demands attention."[5] In this chapter, therefore, I contend that ANA preachers require a bicultural or "hybrid" hermeneutic that takes into consideration both Western and Eastern cultures and philo-

---

2   See Matthew D. Kim, *A Little Book for New Preachers: Why and How to Study Homiletics* (Downers Grove, IL: IVP Academic, 2020), 55.

3   William W. Klein, Craig L. Blomberg, and Robert L. Hubbard Jr., *Introduction to Biblical Interpretation,* 3rd ed. (Grand Rapids: Zondervan, 2017), 56.

4   E. Randolph Richards and Brandon J. O'Brien, *Misreading Scripture with Western Eyes: Removing Cultural Blinders to Better Understand the Bible* (Downers Grove, IL: InterVarsity, 2012), 12.

5   See Jin Young Choi, "Asian/Asian American Interpretation," in *The Oxford Encyclopedia of the Bible and Gender Studies,* ed. Julia M. O'Brien (NY: Oxford University Press, 2014), 3.

sophies. ANA preachers read and interpret Scripture with a unique lens. We need a contextual hermeneutic of our own that will inform our homiletic.

DO WE REALLY NEED AN
ANA HERMENEUTIC?

But first, you may be wondering if there is a universal approach for interpreting Scripture. Do ANA pastors really interpret Scripture all that differently from members of other cultures? Wouldn't a racially sensitive hermeneutic be susceptible to "liberal" or "misguided" interpretations? Put more strongly: Aren't contextual theologies heretical theologies?

When one considers interpretive methods with respect to ANA contexts, some, inside and outside of ANA circles, might argue that there is no difference or should be no difference between how ANA pastors interpret Scripture and any other cultural group. "The gospel is the gospel in every context," they say, and it's true: the gospel never changes. The gospel is, in simple terms, the good news of Jesus Christ: his perfect and sacrificial life, death, burial, resurrection, ascension, and return. And while the historical-grammatical method of biblical interpretation taught in Western/North American evangelical seminaries stresses things with universal applicability like understanding biblical history, grammatical study, and literary context, it is also primarily or even exclusively filtered through a Western/Eurocentric/North American/white evangelical lens.[6] White evangelical approaches to Scripture, in other words, represent the norm in North America. Amos Yong observes that "evangelical theological tendencies generally urge a universalistic horizon, and in this paradigm, there is no need to articulate Asian, Asian [North] American or other cultural and ethnic perspectives since

---

6   Matthew D. Kim, *Preaching with Cultural Intelligence: Understanding the People Who Hear Our Sermons* (Grand Rapids: Baker Academic, 2017), 15–16.

these are all subsumed within the biblical framework when read in an evangelical [white] way."[7]

As a result of this universalizing tendency, some white evangelical interpreters consider ethnic or non-white hermeneutics as suspicious, uncritical, and even promulgating heresy. By virtue of being in the majority culture, white evangelicals can claim a culture-free, attachment-free, baggage-free, and disclaimer-free understanding of theology and hermeneutics. Yet all readers of Scripture (including whites) interpret the text through their own cultural lenses that can "blind us to interpretations that the original audience and readers in other cultures see quite naturally."[8] Ethnic minorities trained in Western/North American seminaries often adhere to Western/ Eurocentric/white models of hermeneutics.[9]

In light of this situation, do we really need an ANA hermeneutic? Absolutely! ANAs who have been taught in Western/North American seminaries have too often functioned, in the words of sociologist Mia Tuan, as if settling for the title of "honorary whites" was the only option.[10] The truth is, however, that we were never meant to purely replicate Western/white interpretative methods—as if Western/ white interpreters do not wear their own set of culturally determined lenses. Rather, we should have our own culturally nuanced approaches to Scripture interpretation and application while still completely upholding a high view of Scripture. God has uniquely created us as ANAs, and I am arguing here for a faithful interpretation of Scripture that also includes greater racial and ethnic awareness and sensitivity. For non-ANAs, I am asking you to consider your ANA listeners' cultures more intentionally.

---

7   Amos Yong, "Asian American Evangelical Theology," in *Global Theology in Evangelical Perspective: Exploring the Contextual Nature of Theology and Mission*, ed. Jeffrey P. Greenman and Gene L. Green (Downers Grove, IL: IVP Academic, 2012), 205.

8   Richards and O'Brien, *Misreading Scripture with Western Eyes*, 15.

9   Amos Yong, *The Future of Evangelical Theology: Soundings from the Asian American Diaspora* (Downers Grove, IL: IVP Academic, 2014), 102.

10   Mia Tuan, *Forever Foreigners or Honorary Whites? The Asian Ethnic Experience Today* (New Brunswick, NJ: Rutgers University Press, 1999).

Again, please do not misunderstand me. I affirm that the original biblical author intended a particular and specific meaning, and preachers attempt to discern what that meaning is with assistance from the Holy Spirit. At the same time, I want to acknowledge that ANAs will not always interpret the Bible in the exact same way or with the same emphases as white North Americans because the cultural lenses we wear are not the same shade and sometimes not even the same color.

Calling for an ANA hermeneutic is not the same as questioning ANAs' allegiance and fidelity to the Bible. Many ANA scholars and preachers clearly uphold the centrality and authority of Scripture. Timothy Tseng, a respected ANA Bible scholar and pastor, reassures us that ANAs "reiterate our conviction that the Bible is the marrow of Protestant theology. The Bible is the essential core around which life, death, creation, and eternity revolves. ... It is the template that molds our attitudes and life decisions."[11] Both Daniel and I espouse biblical inerrancy and infallibility without reservation. We believe that there is a single meaning in the text that the divine and human authors intended and that the gospel message does not change.[12] The hermeneutical question I want to explore in this chapter, however, is this: What can different ethnic groups learn from each other as we interpret Scripture? I believe interpreting Scripture from only a Western/Euro-American evangelical theological framework omits necessary consideration of a bicultural or even multicultural ANA existence. It disregards God's creativity and his plan for and celebration of ethnic and cultural diversity.

Contextualization, when done appropriately, is not hazardous to evangelical Christianity. Rather, it is imperative for interpreting Scripture faithfully in view of ethnic and cultural variances that cannot and should not be ignored. Defining and constructing an

---

11 Timothy Tseng, foreword in *Conversations: Asian American Evangelical Theologies in Formation*, ed. D. J. Chuang and Timothy Tseng (Washington, DC: L2 Foundation, 2006), i.

12 See Kim, *Preaching with Cultural Intelligence*, 34–36.

evangelical ANA hermeneutic will be complex and involves integrating seemingly incompatible Western and Eastern values and philosophies. I want to progress beyond traditional binary understandings of conservative-liberal interpretations to highlight the fact that contextualized biblical interpretation can remain conservative in its approach but also seek to ask questions of the text that ANA listeners are asking. In the next few sections, I'll identify and name some Western influences on biblical interpretation and then move on to consider Eastern influences. I will conclude this chapter with a more balanced and textured strategy and template for ANA biblical interpretation.

WESTERN HERMENEUTICS

ANA preachers trained in Western/North American seminaries will often subscribe to one of a number of hermeneutical approaches: for example, a historical-grammatical model, a canonical model, a literary model, a rhetorical model, an African American model or another racially/culturally sensitive model, a philosophical model, or a theological model.[13] Others might align with denominationally supported interpretive models. While I do not have the space here to explore every hermeneutical model that might have influenced ANA preachers, I would like to draw attention to two dominant and influential strands of Western interpretation: the redemptive-historic hermeneutic (common in Reformed and Presbyterian denominations) and the law/gospel (Lutheran) understanding of hermeneutics. Let me briefly unpack both of these Western/North American interpretive approaches to see how they have made an impact on ANA pastors and their way of interpreting the text.

First, many ANA preachers who come from Reformed or Presbyterian backgrounds read Scripture through a redemptive-historic perspective. Leading advocates like Bryan Chapell, Sidney Greidanus, Timothy Keller, Julius Kim, and others would call this a

---

13   See Bailey, *Hermeneutics for Preaching*.

Christ-centered hermeneutic.[14] This approach involves a theological commitment to reading the text in a way that emphasizes the overarching metanarrative of Scripture, preaching about the person and work of Jesus Christ, or even including the gospel message in every sermon. Keller says: "You want to show listeners Jesus himself and all that he came to do for us. To preach the gospel every time is to preach Christ every time, from every passage. Only if we preach Christ every time can we show how the whole Bible fits together."[15] Christ-centered sermons heavily underline our inability to be sanctified or live out biblical commands without a proper acknowledgment of what Christ has done for us. A common downside of such messages, however, is that the applications begin to sound alike because the sermon often leads to the statement that Jesus has paid the ultimate price and done it all for us. As such, the preacher may not always provide a robust consideration of the biblical author's original purpose and application for his readers and, in turn, may give short shrift to considering what it means for today's listeners.

A second prevalent hermeneutic for ANA preachers is what is referred to as the law/gospel approach. This understands every scriptural text as revealing the law/sin in the world, clarifying that we cannot possibly fulfill/rectify it on our own and imparting the gospel message of grace, which shows us what Christ has done on our behalf and the hope he gives to the world. Growing up in a very conservative and, at times, legalistic Korean American Presbyterian church environment, I heard countless sermons with an overemphasis on the law and our disobedience to it. We often heard shame-laden

---

14   See Bryan Chapell, *Christ-Centered Preaching: Redeeming the Expository Sermon*, 3rd ed., (Grand Rapids: Baker Academic, 2018); Sidney Greidanus, *Preaching Christ from the Old Testament: A Contemporary Hermeneutical Method* (Grand Rapids: Eerdmans, 1999); Timothy Keller, *Preaching: Communicating Faith in an Age of Skepticism* (New York: Viking 2015); and Julius J. Kim, *Preaching the Whole Counsel of God: Design and Deliver Gospel-Centered Sermons* (Grand Rapids: Zondervan, 2015). For a resource on the intersection of hermeneutics and homiletics, see Scott M. Gibson and Matthew D. Kim, eds., *Homiletics and Hermeneutics: Four Views on Preaching Today* (Grand Rapids: Baker Academic, 2018).

15   Keller, *Preaching*, 56–57.

sermons with only occasional sprinkles of grace. It stands out in my memory how discouraging and weighty these sermons were for my soul as they left me feeling hyper-guilty over my sin and feeling like I could never please the Lord. I often left Sunday worship feeling spiritually beat up, even less hopeful than when I entered the sanctuary. The consistent pounding of the waves of guilt and shame washed over me each Sunday.

The opposite extreme can also occur where preachers hyperemphasize the gospel and grace, leaving listeners with a sense that no action is required. Seeking to present a more balanced understanding, advocates of law/gospel sermons like Paul Scott Wilson envision a structure as four pages of a sermon: "Page One is trouble in the biblical text; Page Two is trouble in our world; Page Three is grace in the biblical text; and Page Four is grace in our world."[16]

While there are other Western hermeneutical methods, such as Anglican, Baptist, Methodist, or Pentecostal, the two mentioned above in particular hold sway over many ANA preachers. It's of central importance to identify your hermeneutic, which inevitably shapes your homiletic.[17] As I've stated differently elsewhere, "Every preacher preaches out of an articulated or unarticulated perspective. The perspective might be methodological, theoretical, philosophical, cultural, sociological, or theological."[18] What is the hermeneutic that guides your interpretation of Scripture? Can you clearly name and define it? In most cases, this hermeneutic has been from a Western perspective only. To form a hermeneutic that's both North American and Asian, let's consider some of the "forgotten" Asian cultural and religious influences that may affect your ANA listeners' Scripture interpretation.

---

16   Paul Scott Wilson, *The Four Pages of the Sermon: A Guide to Biblical Preaching*, rev. and updated ed. (Nashville: Abingdon, 2018), 4.

17   See Gibson and Kim, *Homiletics and Hermeneutics,* xi.

18   Gibson and Kim, *Homiletics and Hermeneutics,* xi.

EASTERN HERMENEUTICS

A number of Eastern hermeneutics are widespread whether we are conscious of them or not. Here, I would like to reference several of them and bring them to your attention. I have taken the liberty to name these "Eastern hermeneutics," though they may be known under different guises.

A Confucian Hermeneutic

Most East Asian cultures are defined by the moral philosophies and codes of Confucius (551–479 BC). Confucius taught members of societies how to have harmony with one another through a system of hierarchy and ethical living.[19] His philosophy and teachings especially penetrated China, Japan, Vietnam, and Korea. Two moral virtues stand out in Confucius's teaching: *jen,* or humaneness, and *hsiao,* filial piety, which is showing great respect to parents, elders, and ancestors.[20] We see remnants of filial piety even in second, third, and further generations of ANA congregations where showing deference in leadership and decision-making is common based on age.

A number of years ago, my wife and I had dinner with Tim and Kathy Keller at Scott and Rhonda Gibson's home when Keller was giving a preaching lectureship at Gordon-Conwell Theological Seminary. During the conversation, he asked me why it was that so often the Asian American members at his church did not want to serve as elders. I explained that even among second and later generations of Asian Americans, Confucianism and ageism remain fixtures in the culture. To serve as an elder would mean not just that one was spiritually mature, but also chronologically older as well. To serve the church as an elder in one's twenties, thirties, or even forties would seem premature.

---

19   Thomas A. Tweed and Stephen Prothero, eds., *Asian Religions in America: A Documentary History* (New York: Oxford University Press, 1999), 21.

20   Tweed and Prothero, *Asian Religions in America,* 21.

A Confucian hermeneutical lens in certain ways mirrors law/gospel hermeneutics, where sermons can often sound moralistic or legalistic. Jeffrey Jue compares the two systems of thought in this manner:

> Much of evangelical preaching can be described as moralistic preaching, without a proper understanding of the grace of God given through Jesus Christ. In some ways, Asian culture is particularly suited for moralistic preaching. Asian culture has been heavily shaped by Confucianism, with its goal of moral perfection, and it's very easy to exchange Confucian moral standards for Christian ones.[21]

Sometimes ANA preachers interpret the text in view of tacit Confucian philosophies with heavy emphases placed on collective harmony in the church, behavioral modification or moralism, and improving or saving one's face. The concept of "saving face," or *ch'emyon* in Korean, lends itself to collectivistic thinking where an individual's behavior either honors or shames the entire nuclear and extended families.[22] Consequently, rather than being motivated to become more like Christ and pursue holiness, a Confucian hermeneutic might simply address how one acts in such a way to "save face" for one's family or even his or her church family, which can reflect another form of moralistic preaching.

A Pilgrimage, Marginalization, and Liberation Hermeneutic

Another common way to understand ANA hermeneutics is through the lenses of pilgrimage, marginalization, and liberation. These descriptors are distinct from each other and yet intertwined. In the

---

21 Jeffery Jue, "Does the Asian-American Church Need an Adjusted Gospel?," 9 Marks (website), September 25, 2015, https://www.9marks.org/article/does-the-asian-american-church-need-an-adjusted-gospel.

22 See Kim, *Preaching to Second Generation Korean Americans,* 34.

Korean immigrant Christian context as well as in other marginalized Asian ethnic groups, the immigrant church has provided a sense of familiarity and respite from a foreign American culture and various necessary linguistic, cultural, and social functions such as: "(1) fellowship for Korean immigrants, (2) maintenance of the Korean cultural tradition, (3) social services for church members and the Korean community as a whole, and (4) social status and social positions for adult immigrants."[23]

Asian immigrants have interpreted the Bible as pilgrims who are sojourning through life in a temporary residence whose ultimate destination is not North America, but rather a heavenly city. Due to being marginalized by the majority culture, Asian immigrant theologians like Jung Young Lee have also read Scripture through the lens of marginalization and alienation with residual feelings of oppression and isolation, having been made to feel inferior and like an "other."[24] To counteract feelings of marginalization, some have taken the onus to seek liberation from one's oppressors. Sometimes the hermeneutic of pilgrimage, marginalization, and liberation have trickled down to second-, third-, fourth-, and fifth-generation ANAs who desperately seek an acknowledgment of equality with members of the majority culture and the ability to influence them.

A Postcolonial Hermeneutic

Depending on when an Asian person arrives in North America and from which country they have emigrated (e.g., formerly colonized Asian countries like India, the Philippines, and Korea), a postcolonial reading may be a factor in their hermeneutic. Postcolonial readings are traditionally less common for members of East Asian cultures,

---

23 Pyong Gap Min, "The Structure and Social Functions of Korean Immigrant Churches in the United States," *International Migration Review* 26:4 (Winter 1992): 1370.

24 Jung Young Lee, *Marginality: The Key to Multicultural Theology* (Minneapolis: Fortress, 1995), 112. Woosung Calvin Choi has put an optimistic spin on marginality in his book, *Preaching to Multiethnic Congregation: Positive Marginality as a Homiletical Paradigm* (New York: Peter Lang, 2015).

although this interpretive view has trickled in. Daniel Martino explains that a postcolonial hermeneutic recognizes that in the past "biblical texts were often used and misused to justify the interaction of the colonial enterprise with the colonized."[25] This approach understands that the relationship between the colonizer (e.g., England, the United States, and Japan) and the colonized has often been brittle and antagonistic. For instance, a common Scripture passage mishandled and abused by a postcolonial reading is Joshua 1:2, where God commands Joshua to cross the Jordan River and take possession of the land "from the desert to Lebanon, and from the great river, the Euphrates—all the Hittite country—to the Mediterranean Sea in the west" (Josh 1:4). Depending on one's position as either the colonizer or the one being colonized, the text will be interpreted quite differently.

Postcolonial theory is rather complicated and expansive in scope. It can mean different things to different people.[26] In various circles, a postcolonial hermeneutic of Scripture may be concerned with issues of control, hegemony, race, politics, economics, identity, equity, poverty, or other relevant topics. With a postcolonial reading, any Bible passage that addresses power and the powerless can take on a different meaning for the interpreter. A more positive biblical example concerns the book of Nehemiah, where the governor gets angry at the exploitation of his people and employs his resources and influence for the common good (Neh 5:6). Depending on one's ethnic and cultural context, postcolonial interpretations may be one factor in the interpretive process.

A Blessing Hermeneutic

Another hermeneutic that pervades cross sections of ANA preachers includes a hyper-emphasis on material and spiritual blessings. Although it can sound similar to the prosperity gospel in the West,

---

25   Daniel J. Martino, "Postcolonial Biblical Hermeneutics: Interpreting with a Genuine Attunement to Otherness," *Analecta Hermeneutica*, vol. 4 (2012), 7.

26   Wonhee Anne Joh, *Heart of the Cross: A Postcolonial Christology* (Louisville: Westminster John Knox, 2006), xx.

Asian preachers with this hermeneutic have been influenced by Shamanism, in which a shaman priest dispenses various kinds of blessings. In certain Korean immigrant churches, shamanistic sermons are preached about receiving all kinds of earthly blessings.[27] Eunjoo Mary Kim, a first-generation Korean American homiletics professor, observes: "Korean American preaching has catered to this prevailing secular idea of the American Dream ... [with its] present-centered, individualistic materialism, and have ignored the future-oriented communal and holistic aspects of the blessing of God."[28]

The desire for blessings is, of course, not unique to ANA Christians alone. The Bible is replete with many examples of blessing language from God the Father. Yet pockets of ANA preachers read into the Scripture a prosperity or blessing theology in an unhealthy, exaggerated, or forced way. A number of sermons that I heard growing up in the Korean immigrant church focused on *bok,* or blessings. Sometimes this blessing hermeneutic unintentionally communicates a quid pro quo or this-for-that theology, where if we do something for God, God will bless us twofold or even a hundredfold.

ANA CONTEXTUALIZATION

To this point, we have briefly explored common Western and Eastern approaches to hermeneutics. In the remaining sections of this chapter, I will outline a hybrid contextualized hermeneutic that considers both worlds and is faithful to Scripture and yet culturally sensitive for ANA listeners.

In certain evangelical circles, contextualization is a dirty word. Its meanings are, at times, pejorative and associated with liberalism,

---

27   Tae-Ju Moon, "The Korean American Dream and the Blessings of Hananim (God)," in *The Global God: Multicultural Evangelical Views of God,* ed. Aida Besancon Spencer and William David Spencer (Grand Rapids: Baker, 1998), 238, 242. See also Kim, *Preaching to Second Generation Korean Americans,* 32–33.

28   Eunjoo Mary Kim, "A Korean American Perspective: Singing a New Song in a Strange Land," in *Preaching Justice: Ethnic and Cultural Perspectives,* ed. Christine M. Smith (Eugene, OR: Wipf & Stock, 2008), 104.

colonization, colonialism, syncretism, uncritical concerns for social justice, and more. However, in simple terms, to contextualize is "to place (something, such as a word or activity) in a context."[29] Due to some evangelicals' suspicion of contextualization, Amos Yong observes that "ethnic identities are minimized as having no more than biological significance, and historical and cultural aspects of Asian identity are accepted only as accidental to identity in Christ."[30] Contextualization in view of biblical exegesis involves interpreting Scripture through the lens and experience of someone who is different from us—whatever those differences may be.

Stephen Bevans explains that contextualization considers the following types of human experiences:

> First, context involves the experiences of a person's or group's personal life: the experiences of success, failure, births, deaths, relationships, etc. ... Second, personal or communal experience is possible only within the context of culture. ... Third, we can speak of context in terms of a person's or a community's social location. ... Finally, the notion of present experience or context involves the reality of social change.[31]

I commend Bevans's observation that contextualization "is not something on the fringes of the theological enterprise. It is at the very center of what it means to do theology in today's world. Contextualization, in other words, is a theological imperative."[32] To

---

29   See "Contextualization," *Merriam-Webster's Dictionary,* accessed October 30, 2019, https://www.merriam-webster.com/dictionary/contextualize.

30   Yong, *The Future of Evangelical Theology,* 105.

31   Stephen Bevans, "Living between Gospel and Context: Models for a Missional Church in North America," in *Confident Witness—Changing World: Rediscovering the Gospel in North America,* ed. Craig Van Gelder (Grand Rapids: Eerdmans, 1999), 144–45.

32   Stephen Bevans, *Models of Contextual Theology* (Maryknoll, NY: Orbis, 1992), 10.

contextualize God's word, as we understand it, is not to alter the meaning of the text, but rather to interpret it in such a way that hearers can understand and grapple with its meaning and apply it in a relevant manner.

One of the goals for those preaching in ANA pulpits is to take the root of the word "context," which "denotes interwovenness or braiding," and remember that it "is neither selective nor fixed, but dynamic and interactive."[33] We are engaging many different aspects of ANA listeners' lives—their Asian culture(s) as well as American/Canadian cultures. Jeffrey Jue contends that "to contextualize the Bible is to understand the text in light of the specific cultural experiences of Asian [North] Americans. Essentially this is accomplished by bridging the ancient world of the text and the modern context of Asian [North] Americans."[34] As such, we must recognize the significance that ethnic identity plays in ANA churches (see chapter 1). In order to engage effectively with ANAs from the pulpit, preachers should actively explore and evaluate their listeners' ethnic and cultural identities and identify the complexities that arise from living in two or more discrete cultures.

A second goal for ANA preachers involves assisting listeners in combating the reality of social oppression, power dynamics, and accentuating the need for social change. As discussed earlier, ANAs continue to experience marginalization from the dominant society despite their US or Canadian citizenship, facility with the English language, or adherence to many North American cultural norms. Our Asian countenance is perpetually equated with foreignness and otherness. In addition, ANAs must continually navigate the Eastern philosophies and values preserved by their parents.

In this context, what holds together an ANA hermeneutic?

---

33   Eunjoo Mary Kim, *Preaching in an Age of Globalization* (Louisville: Westminster John Knox, 2010), 20.

34   Jue, *Conversations*, 107.

THE VOWELS OF HERMENEUTICS

Mark Allan Powell once did a study with US/Western seminary students on the prodigal son story in Luke 15.[35] The first group of twelve students, when asked to recount the story in their own words, failed to mention Jesus' detail of the famine in verse 14: "After he had spent everything, there was a severe famine in that whole country, and he began to be in need." This led Powell to do some further research. He then conducted a study with one hundred American students and found that only six mentioned the famine. His third study was done with fifty Russian students in St. Petersburg. In that Eastern European context, forty-two out of fifty people mentioned the famine.[36]

Powell later brought the same prodigal son story survey to Tanzania in East Africa. With approximately fifty Tanzanian seminarians, Powell asked, "Why does the young man end up starving in the pigpen?" He expected to see replies concerning the famine or squandering money. But to his surprise, about 80 percent responded, "Because no one gave him anything to eat." This small detail is found in verse 16: "He longed to fill his stomach with the pods that the pigs were eating, *but no one gave him anything*" (emphasis added). Powell concludes that the social location of the reader does seem to matter significantly in how one reads, remembers, and interprets a text.[37]

Like Powell's students, ANA readers of Scripture and preachers of the word read the text with our own ethnic/cultural perspective. The interpretations that arise from this perspective will land somewhere on a spectrum from Asian to North American values, beliefs, and assumptions. To help ANA preachers consider the challenges of interpreting Scripture for ANA listeners, I suggest using a

---

35   Thanks to Jeffrey Arthurs at Gordon-Conwell Theological Seminary for sharing this reference.

36   See Mark Allan Powell, *What Do They Hear? Bridging the Gap Between Pulpit & Pew* (Nashville: Abingdon, 2007), 14–18.

37   Powell, *What Do They Hear?*, 26–27.

hermeneutical approach with five steps that begin with the vowels of the English language.

Vowels hold words together in English and in many other languages, and we might also say that vowels can hold together the process of hermeneutics.[38] In their *Introduction to Biblical Interpretation Workbook,* Klein, Blomberg, and Hubbard Jr. state, "Accurate Bible study must proceed on the basis that we have read the text carefully. We can't move on to interpretation and application until we master the first step of observation. We must see what is actually in the text and not read into it or assume ideas that are not really there."[39] They articulate a three-part process of hermeneutics using the vowels O (observation), I (interpretation), and A (application). To this method, I would like to add experience and understanding to round out the O-E-U-I-A process of hermeneutics: observation, experience, understanding, interpretation, and application.

As I've already suggested, everyone interprets Scripture from his or her own perspective and experience. This perspective and experience can be formed by one's gender, ethnicity, culture, generation, vocation, socioeconomic class, political views, or other attributes. While we commit ourselves to interpreting the text through the biblical author's lens as best as we can, to interpret Scripture faithfully and systematically in our ANA context, we may try walking through the vowels of hermeneutics.

To help further define this approach, I want to walk through the steps of interpretation while looking at Luke 14:25–27. Along the way, I will look for similarities and differences between ANA cultures and Ancient Near Eastern (ANE) or biblical cultures. From Jesus' mouth, these words have caused ANA immigrant parents a

---

38   Kim presents a pathway for cross-cultural hermeneutics using the acronym HABIT (Historical, grammatical, and literary context; Author's cultural context; Big idea of the text; Interpret in your context; and Theological presuppositions) in *Preaching with Cultural Intelligence,* 31–44.

39   William W. Klein, Craig L. Blomberg, and Robert L. Hubbard Jr., *Introduction to Biblical Interpretation Workbook* (Grand Rapids: Zondervan, 2017), 13.

lot of anguish. If pressed, many may wish Luke had simply left this one out of his Gospel:

> Large crowds were traveling with Jesus, and turning
> to them he said: "If anyone comes to me and does not
> hate father and mother, wife and children, brothers and
> sisters—yes, even their own life—such a person cannot
> be my disciple. And whoever does not carry their cross
> and follow me cannot be my disciple."

1. Observation

What are some general observations that we can make regarding this text from both Asian and North American cultures? Jesus seems to be speaking in binary terms. You either love him or not. A key word in this text would be "hate." What does Jesus mean by hate my parents and siblings? How can I hate my family? How can I hate myself? Why would Jesus ask me to hate anyone? Isn't the second greatest commandment to love my neighbor as myself? Isn't this dangerous, since suicide attempts and successful suicides continue to rise even among Christians?[40]

It would be helpful to know that Jesus appears to be using a literary device called hyperbole or exaggeration to make his point. It's not that Jesus wants us to literally hate our family, but rather that Jesus expects us to love him and obey him more than we love and obey our family—and this is where it hurts—even if it means leaving them behind. While disowning one's children for embracing Christianity is probably more common among Muslim families, Asian families still experience this alienation when the Christian life competes with Asian/Confucian values. It would be helpful for ANA preachers to acknowledge some of the various hardships raised by this passage.

---

40   See Karen Mason, *Preventing Suicide: A Handbook for Pastors, Chaplains and Pastoral Counselors* (Downers Grove, IL: InterVarsity, 2014).

2. Experience

Next, what experiences do ANAs have in common with the biblical characters/God's instructions in the text? In what ways do they differ? How does the text inform, shape, or correct North American values, Asian values, or both? From a young age, ANAs frequently view life through the lens of honor and shame, as noted earlier. Guilt and shame are often two sides of the same coin. As Jeffrey Jue observes, however, we must not always think in completely binary terms:

> I have seen some pastors and theologians insist that the gospel, when presented to Asians and Asian [North] Americans, should be framed solely by the notion of shame before God, excluding any discussion of guilt. Put simply, they claim that guilt is a Western cultural characteristic, while shame is more of an Eastern cultural characteristic. ... In my opinion, however, you cannot preach the gospel without discussing the guilt of all sinners before the judgment of God (Romans 6:23). And guilt is not the same thing as shame. Moreover, guilt is not a foreign cultural concept for Asians. ... Again, this is a subtle form of stereotyping that requires careful attention.[41]

For many ANAs, this passage contradicts almost everything they have learned about honoring parents and valuing the family unit above all else. At the same time, Jesus challenges our sense of individualism and love of self where we must lay down our own life if we want to be his disciple.

This text challenges both Asian and North American values, and the word of God trumps both. My goal in preaching this text would

---

41 See Jeffrey Jue, "Does the Asian-American Church Need an Adjusted Gospel?," 9 Marks (website), September 25, 2015, https://www.9marks.org/article/does-the-asian-american-church-need-an-adjusted-gospel/.

be to acknowledge the sheer difficulty for ANAs to do what Jesus asks. Don't gloss too quickly over this tension. Ask probing questions of your listeners and get them to intentionally consider their Asian side. At the same time, acknowledge that Jesus' teaching goes against the East Asian value of family being put on a pedestal as well as the North American value of rugged individualism. I would commend all of my listeners' hard work to get to where they are and recognize what it means to follow Christ in light of this.

3. Understanding

Some might refer to understanding as one's preunderstanding, which is "all of our preconceived notions and understandings that we bring to the text, which have been formulated, both consciously and subconsciously, before we actually study the text in detail. ... The danger here is for those who assume that their preunderstanding is always correct."[42] What concepts, metaphors, images, details, and cultural variances will my ANA listeners understand or preunderstand differently from my perspective, which may have an impact on how I explain, prove, and apply the text?

ANAs have various preconceived understandings of what it means to be Jesus' disciples. For example, from a young age, many teenagers in my youth group heard both verbally and indirectly from our youth pastors that if you really want to follow Jesus, you need to go to seminary and serve God full-time by becoming a missionary or a pastor. I remember at the 1993 Urbana missions conference at the University of Illinois at Urbana-Champaign almost every member of my youth group who attended the conference dedicated their lives to full-time missions. Years later, not a single person had followed through on that commitment. I am the only one from that youth group who is now serving in any kind of full-time vocational

---

42   J. Scott Duvall and J. Daniel Hays, *Grasping God's Word: A Hands-On Approach to Reading, Interpreting, and Applying the Bible,* 3rd ed. (Grand Rapids: Zondervan, 2012), 139–40. See also Kim, *Preaching with Cultural Intelligence,* 32–33.

ministry. For some students, they went from radical commitment to serving the Lord in high school to leaving the faith during their college years. Certain ANAs have understood discipleship to be an all-or-nothing type faith (full-time vocational ministry or bust). In ANA contexts, we need to do a better job of cultivating both full-time ministry servants and those who serve God in the marketplace. Ministry is not accomplished within the binary of either being in full-time ministry or a secular occupation. All ANAs can serve God faithfully wherever God places them. This encouragement needs to be accentuated from the ANA pulpit.

4. Interpretation

As I have developed elsewhere, I encourage us to interpret the text in light of our particular cultural context.[43] Three interpretive considerations include asking what assumptions, conflicts, and questions our listeners may have as they read the text. Depending on where the ANA listener is on the Asian and North American sides of the spectrum, he or she will have varying assumptions, conflicts, and questions.

For instance, an Asian cultural assumption/conflict might be that it is impossible to hate one's family and one's own life in order to follow Jesus. A North American cultural assumption/conflict may be less concerned with the family and more concerned about what Jesus says in verse 27 with respect to carrying one's cross (because he or she may be more individual-minded). Some questions ANAs might ask if they see themselves primarily as Asian include: "How does one actually hate one's family and self?" and "What does that look like on a daily basis?" ANAs with a more North American mindset might wonder, "How long and in what specific situations must I deny myself and carry my cross? Does this pertain to each and every aspect of my life? If so, how do I apply this?" Both sides of the spectrum

---

43   See Kim, *Preaching with Cultural Intelligence*, 42–43.

require some investigative legwork, depending on our knowledge of the congregation.

5. *Application*

All of these vowels lead to one of the most challenging aspects of interpretation: application. We may ask the same question in a myriad of ways: How do we live out biblical instruction and teaching? How does this text change my life? What action does the text require of us? And specifically, the ANA preacher should ask: What does that look like for an ANA listener? What does it mean for us to follow Christ as ANA persons?

A primary application for this text is counting the cost. There are inherent costs in following Jesus. In fact, following Jesus costs everything. This text can apply to taking a new career path or being more Christlike in our current workplace, personal suffering or having our family suffer for Christ in some way, laying down our comforts, diminishing the importance of our hard-earned educations and careers, minimizing our status and prestige, and setting aside our pride. It may mean giving up personal dreams. In the rest of this passage, Jesus gives two examples of evaluating the costs involved (an example from construction and another from war) before we make a critical decision. Then he concludes by saying that salt should be thrown out if it loses its saltiness.

A second application (a corollary of the first) might regard sacrificing familial relationships. In our sermon, we might address the genuine and loving relationships that we have with our parents and siblings and how this text may affect this relationship. Following Jesus cost our friend, Tom Lin, president of InterVarsity Christian Fellowship, his relationship with his parents. Lin experienced this after completing his undergraduate degree at Harvard. Going to work for IVCF meant fundraising for his salary, which was a great source of shame for his Taiwanese/Chinese-cultured parents. Eventually, it cost Tom his relationship with his father and mother for quite some time. Some Korean parents, for instance, prefer their Christian children to marry even non-Christians who are ethnically Korean for the sake of preserving the Korean heritage in the family line. Following Christ may involve marrying a Christian who is not of the same ethnicity to the chagrin of our ethnocentric parents.

Third, we might consider the implications of the cross and what it means to carry our own cross. The cross can mean something different from an Asian perspective versus a North American one. For a person holding an Asian worldview, the cross may call to mind a physical representation of suffering. While they may not physically hit or starve themselves like the ascetics of old, the cross represents a physical type of suffering for certain Asian psyches. Part of this correlation relates to the suffering taught by Buddha in Buddhism and Hinduism. We will speak more of this later in chapter 3. For a North American, the cross is less of a physical descriptor and more representative of emotional and/or psychological suffering. A North American may not relate to Paul's forty lashes minus one, but he or she may relate to experiencing abandonment, shipwreck, or torn relationships based on one's ministry beliefs and practices.

CONCLUSION

In this chapter, I have made the case that it's not enough to interpret Scripture only from a Western perspective when preaching to ANA listeners. We want to make a concerted effort to interpret the Bible using a hybrid hermeneutic. While I have only touched the surface here, I hope I have raised some important considerations for your hermeneutical process. I know that the approach I have proposed will take time to integrate into your sermon preparation; after all, interpreting Scripture is challenging enough when considering only one cultural perspective. But the task before you requires some measure of Asian *and* North American cultural awareness and sensitivity. As you become more familiar with your congregation, you will appreciate these ethnic and cultural dimensions more and will more readily come up with ideas as you walk through the five vowels of hermeneutics. None of us can interpret for everyone, but we can attempt to do so in an intentional manner.

In the next chapter, we will take a closer look at ANA theologies and how they factor into the preaching task as well.

QUESTIONS FOR REFLECTION
AND DISCUSSION

1. In what ways do the biblical authors' cultural context overlap with or diverge from Asian culture and North American culture?

2. What is your default hermeneutical lens (e.g., Reformed, Christ-centered, Wesleyan/Arminian, law/gospel, big idea, God-centered, etc.)? How did this become your default lens?

3. What areas of Asian hermeneutics do you consider helpful for interpreting Scripture?

4. What types of hermeneutics are prevalent in your congregation (e.g., Confucian, pilgrimage, marginalization, liberation, postcolonial, blessing, etc.)?

5. To what extent is your congregation influenced by Confucian ideals (e.g., filial piety, importance of education, ageism, collectivism, etc.)? What difference does this make in how you approach a text?

6. To what extent is your congregation influenced by Western ideals (e.g., equality, equity, individualism, freedom, meritocracy, etc.)? What difference does this make in how you approach a text?

7. What would an ANA hermeneutic look like in your church?

CHAPTER
THREE

Matthew D. Kim

ASIAN NORTH AMERICAN THEOLOGIES

I'm convinced that the majority of our churches are Pharisee factories, and as products of these churches and seminaries, most of us Asian [North] American preachers are Neo-Pharisees, stripping the grace from the gospel and instead promoting subtle forms of legalism and moralism. So we preachers must first have our own DREs (Damascus Road Experiences) where we allow Christ to confront us with our hypocrisy and then strip us of our pretense.

—Ken Fong, senior pastor emeritus,
Evergreen Baptist Church of Los Angeles

Many ethnicities and cultures take great pleasure in naming things after themselves. I still remember the first time I saw a particularly large and appetizing fruit at the Korean grocery store in Koreatown in Chicago. While many Asians would describe this fruit as an "Asian" pear, the Korean grocer had labeled it as a "Korean" pear.

Since people are ethnocentric, it's only natural that ethnic groups claim that the good things in life originated with their people group. There's no harm in taking pride in your own ethnic background as long as it doesn't cause you to reject other backgrounds simply because they are not your own. However, when it comes to evangelical theology, there seems to be only one (Western) theology and a host of pseudo-theologies. Ken Wytsma, a white American of Dutch heritage, in his book, *The Myth of Equality,* describes this power dynamic in Western evangelicalism as the white normative standard where "whiteness became and was ingrained as the bar or canon by which things were evaluated or contrasted. Whiteness became the racial category by which all others were evaluated. ... It also speaks to a complicity in benefiting from racialized systems."[1] The white normative standard perpetuates the view "that real theology transcends culture. ... Thus, theologies that emerge from European and American seminaries are represented as pure and culturally transcendent—even by Asian [North] American theological educators!"[2]

Consequently, theologians call Western theology "theology" without any preceding descriptor because Western/European/North American theologians can differentiate all other theologies using a racial/ethnic label such as African theologies, black theologies, Hispanic/Latino theologies, indigenous theologies, Native American theologies, and in our case, Asian or ANA theologies.

What this suggests is that there has been only one true version of theology, which is a white normative standard version of theology. In response, I want to ask: (1) To whom does theology really belong? (2) Is there a monopoly on theology or a single monotheology? (3) Is there only one theological perspective—a white normative standard theology to which everyone else must assimilate? Or can there be a theology represented by all different ethnic and cultural perspectives—each adding its own unique perspective on who God is? I would propose that there is no pure, culture-free theology. As Daniel Lee contends, "All theologies, speaking from their contexts,

---

1   Ken Wytsma, *The Myth of Equality: Uncovering the Roots of Injustice and Privilege* (Downers Grove, IL: InterVarsity, 2017), 20.

2   Timothy Tseng, foreword in *Conversations: Asian American Evangelical Theologies in Formation,* ed. DJ Chuang and Timothy Tseng (Washington, DC: L2 Foundation, 2006), ii.

will together represent the fullness of what Christianity truly is."[3] We can then think of theology resembling a tapestry or a quilt rather than a blanket made of one material.

For the most part, ANA pastors have adopted a white normative standard theology. For example, a few years ago, an older white pastor of a large congregation asked me why other racial groups aren't as good at assimilating as Asian Americans. The common assumption is that Asians are good at yielding, bending, and bowing to North American norms in order to fit in. As Wytsma notes, "Asian Americans have often been successful within white culture because they approximate it in many respects. When whites look at Asians and feel an affinity with them, it's often on the assumption that Asians seem able to mimic the Protestant work ethic and white values."[4] Put succinctly, it's assumed that ANAs hold completely to a white normative theology without room for discussion.

Yet even second, third, and further generations of ANAs are consciously or subconsciously influenced by the theology of immigrant churches. Some of these churches have traces of Eastern religions such as Buddhism, Hinduism, Shintoism, Taoism, ancestry worship, or others. I will not attempt to unpack here the various religious doctrines and their specific influences on ANA theology. If you are interested in learning more about Asian religions, an abundance of thoughtful literature exists already on those topics.[5]

I also want to acknowledge up front that ANAs hold a wide swath of theological perspectives. They range from conservative, evangelical denominations like Calvinists/Reformed, Presbyterians, Baptists, Arminians/Wesleyans, Lutherans, Pentecostals, dispensationalists, to more mainline and liberal perspectives that embrace, at times, a

---

3   Daniel D. Lee, *Double Particularity: Karl Barth, Contextuality, and Asian American Theology* (Minneapolis: Fortress, 2017), 30.

4   Wytsma, *The Myth of Equality*, 21.

5   For an overview of Asian religions, see Sung Wook Chung, ed., *Christ the One and Only: A Global Affirmation of the Uniqueness of Jesus Christ* (Grand Rapids: Baker Academic, 2005) and Derek Cooper, *Christianity and World Religions: An Introduction to the World's Major Faiths* (Phillipsburg, NJ: P&R, 2013).

hodgepodge of Asian and ANA feminist theology,[6] postcolonial theology,[7] *minjung* theology,[8] waterbuffalo theology,[9] Third-Eye theology,[10] and more. I am not able to comment here on all the varieties of theology held by ANAs. Similarly, the purpose of this chapter is not to discuss exhaustively the literature surrounding Asian and ANA theologies. For that, you might consider reading Simon Chan, *Grassroots Asian Theology: Thinking the Faith from the Ground Up;* Sebastian C. H. Kim, *Christian Theology in Asia;* Sang Hyun Lee, *From a Liminal Place: An Asian American Theology;* Peter C. Phan, *Christianity with an Asian Face: Asian American Theology in the Making;* Amos Yong, *The Future of Evangelical Theology: Soundings from the Asian American Diaspora;* and more.

Much of ANA theology, I admit, derives from more liberal and/or Eastern religious sources, and therefore I understand and appreciate Westerners' suspicions (including mine and Daniel's suspicions as ANA preachers). Please note that we do not accept these ANA theologies wholesale. Nor do I want to suggest that ANA theology should hold the sole voice in theology.

---

6   See, for example, Nami Kim and Wonhee Anne Joh, "Roundtable: Asian/Asian North American Feminist Theologies," *Journal of Feminist Studies in Religion* vol. 31, no. 1 (2015): 107–42; Mihee Kim-Kort, *Making Paper Cranes: Toward an Asian American Feminist Theology* (St. Louis: Chalice, 2012); and Grace Ji-Sun Kim, *The Grace of Sophia: A Korean North American Women's Christology* (Eugene, OR: Wipf & Stock, 2010).

7   Wonhee Anne Joh, *Heart of the Cross: A Postcolonial Christology* (Louisville: Westminster John Knox, 2006).

8   Paul S. Chung, Veli-Matti Kärkkäinen, and Kim Kyoung-Jae, eds., *Asian Contextual Theology for the Third Millennium: A Theology of Minjung in Fourth-Eye Formation* (Eugene, OR: Pickwick, 2007).

9   Kosuke Koyama, *Waterbuffalo Theology* (Maryknoll, NY: Orbis, 1974).

10   C. S. Song maintains that Asian theology is incarnational, but it requires what he calls a "Third Eye." He writes: "Theologians need a 'Third Eye,' namely, a power of perception and insight that enables them to grasp the meaning under the surface of things and phenomena." He continues: "Third-eye theology is therefore an incarnational theology. Such theology allows no barriers to be set up around it to obstruct its view. With faith in the God who acts in history, it ventures into an unknown journey. Jesus Christ and God's salvation in and through him are the center of such a theology." See C. S. Song, *Third-Eye Theology: Theology in Formation in Asian Settings* (Maryknoll, NY: Orbis, 1979), xi, 21.

Instead, our goal is to articulate a contextual theology that takes into consideration both Asian and North American cultures. I want to clarify what ANA evangelical theology looks like today and envision what it may look like going forward in a way that will enhance our vision for ANA homiletics. Much like ANA hermeneutics in chapter 2, an ANA theology must be layered, nuanced, and not simply Western. Below I want to acknowledge a few of the foremost conversations taking place in ANA theology and, more importantly, provide a way forward to help evangelical preachers consider an ANA theology of duality or hybridity that more purposefully and directly shapes their ANA listeners today and in the future.

Amos Yong says: "Asian American evangelical theology has yet to get off the ground even at the beginning of the twenty-first century."[11] Like our African American, Hispanic and Latino American, Native American, and other counterparts, I want to identify and name what an ANA evangelical theology aspires to be and then later, in chapter 5, offer a few reflections on how an ANA evangelical theology might influence our homiletics.

UNDERSTANDING ISMS: PLURALISM, SYNCRETISM, AND EXCLUSIVISM

Christian churches are becoming increasingly penetrated by other religions whether unconsciously or subconsciously. When I served as the senior pastor of an Asian American church, some of my former church members practiced yoga on a regular basis as a form of exercise. "It's just exercise, Pastor Matt!" they would often say to me, grinning from ear to ear.

Yet to my chagrin, at one Friday evening worship service, one church member bowed to another (who also engaged regularly in yoga), pressed her palms together, and said, "Namaste," which means "the god in me sees the god in you." I was shocked and saddened by

---

11 Amos Yong, *The Future of Evangelical Theology: Soundings from the Asian American Diaspora* (Downers Grove, IL: IVP Academic, 2014), 120.

what I had just witnessed. Just exercise? Am I being too old-fashioned? Do I need to get with the times? Yes, yoga can be a wonderful form of exercise to strengthen one's core and improve flexibility. However, steeped as it is in Hindu and Buddhist thought, yoga inevitably communicates philosophies and mantras embedded in these Eastern religions. Could it be putting Christians' faith in peril without their knowledge? I eventually decided to preach a sermon on the pros and cons of practicing yoga as part of a series on "What Do I Believe?" In various Christian congregations, yoga is just one example of a hot topic. How do we make sense of practices like this, which point to the problems of pluralism and syncretism today?

Pluralism is the concept that "all religions [have] equal footing and equal authority."[12] According to pluralists, Christianity is just as valid a religion as Buddhism, Shintoism, Taoism, or any other faith. Pluralists may project the image that all world religions have worth and are worthy of respect. It comes out in statements like "all roads lead to God" or "at least they believe in some kind of religion." Surprisingly, if you did a survey of your church members, you might hear sentiments like this from unexpected people.

Syncretism, as its etymology suggests, is a blending of different religious traditions. It is not the same as contextualization, which is necessary if we are to communicate the gospel in any culture. The difference is flexibility, as Allen Yeh writes:

> How does one discern between contextualization and syncretism, then? This is the difficulty with accepting pluralism as an inherent necessity of the system. Not enough flexibility leads to ghettoization, but too much flexibility leads to syncretism. People who are afraid

---

12   Todd M. Johnson and Cindy M. Wu, *Our Global Families: Christians Embracing Common Identity in a Changing World* (Grand Rapids: Baker Academic, 2015), 125.

of heresy end up absolutizing everything about their expression of their faith, including their culture."[13]

We commonly find glimpses of syncretism with respect to Eastern religions like Buddhism, Confucianism, Shamanism, and Taoism blending with Christianity. Concepts from Buddhism like karma and Shamanistic blessings subconsciously amalgamate with similar Christian teachings.[14]

The third category, which is our perspective in this book, is exclusivism. Exclusivism contends that Christianity is the only true religion by virtue of three characteristics: "(1) the unique authority of Jesus Christ; (2) the death and resurrection of Jesus Christ as the decisive event in human history; and (3) salvation solely through an explicit act of repentance for sin and a proclamation of faith based on Christ's work on the cross."[15] In short, Christianity is an exclusivist religion regardless of one's race, ethnicity, culture, gender, or any other distinction. Part of the challenge in articulating an ANA theology is that we hold fast to exclusivism while trying to make sense of pluralism and syncretism with other Asian religions.

BECOMING SELF-THEOLOGIZING

Missiologist Paul Hiebert encourages churches in the Two-Thirds World (also referred to as the Majority World) to be "self-theologizing."[16] Most ANA pastors who study at evangelical Western seminaries learn theology from a Western perspective as if Westerners do not have their own cultural blinders. As expressed

---

13   Allen Yeh, "Asian Perspectives on Twenty-First-Century Pluralism," in *The Gospel and Pluralism Today: Reassessing Lesslie Newbigin in the 21st Century,* ed. Scott W. Sunquist and Amos Yong (Downers Grove, IL: IVP Academic, 2015), 217.

14   Matthew D. Kim, "Asian-American Preaching," in *The Art and Craft of Biblical Preaching: A Comprehensive Resource for Today's Communicators,* ed. Craig Brian Larson and Haddon Robinson (Grand Rapids: Zondervan, 2005), 200–204.

15   Johnson and Wu, *Our Global Families,* 124.

16   Paul G. Hiebert, *Anthropological Reflections on Missiological Issues* (Grand Rapids: Baker, 1994), 97. See also Yeh, "Asian Perspectives," 220.

earlier, Western theology often constitutes the norm, or "pure theology," while all others (such as African theology, Asian theology, Latin American theology, and Native American theology) are scrutinized and deemed as heresies or aberrations from the real thing.[17] Again, by no means do I advocate here a wholesale acceptance of non-Western theologies. There are numerous tenets in non-Western theology that are heretical, unbiblical, and lack orthodoxy and orthopraxy. Nor am I calling for a coup against Western theology in hopes of colonizing other theologies in favor of an ANA theology.

At the same time, however, to completely dismiss other theologies as unnecessary, profane, and completely heretical would be a significant missed opportunity in understanding the God who designed the world with ethnic and cultural diversity. We should expect to learn about who God is from other ethnic and cultural perspectives, since "the evangelical tradition can be expanded, renewed and developed in dialogue with non-Euro-American conversation partners."[18] The question is: What can we learn from these distinct, ethnic, and cultural theological expressions and from one another?

One of the major struggles among ANAs is the dearth of theological scholarship from an ANA perspective (although it is slowly increasing). Timothy Tseng maintains that:

> Scholars from dominant cultures are not compelled
> to learn about Asian or Asian American Christianity.
> ... [Some believe that] real theology transcends culture.
> Biblical truth cannot intermingle with messy, sinful
> cultural contexts. Consequently, it does not matter
> if we ignore our Asian [North] American stories and
> experiences. After all, these have no value in light of the

---

17   Yeh, "Asian Perspectives," 226.
18   Yong, *The Future of Evangelical Theology*, 98.

pristine truth revealed in Scripture. Left unexplained, however, is how this understanding of a pure theology itself escapes the clutches of Western culture.[19]

My desire is not to dismiss Western theology, but to call for a more fluid conversation concerning the strengths and limitations of each theology that arise out of a specific ethnic and cultural point of view. This includes all theologies, even Western ones.

ANAs are not the only ethnic minority group struggling to find a theological voice. Kenyatta R. Gilbert writes from the black preaching tradition:

> Often is the case, regrettably, that Black scholars reflecting on historically marginalized North American communities shoulder inequitable burdens as writers in a racialized society. Because the theological academy puts a premium on scholarly works modeled after centuries-old norms and dominant paradigms established by Europeans and Euro-American scholars, works that deviate from set norms are generally met with academic suspicion at best, and contempt or indifference at worst.[20]

Similarly, Hispanic and Latino scholars find difficulty gaining theological traction that is ethnically and culturally rooted and nuanced. As Justo González writes, "Both of these central points—incarnation and canon—point to the first issue that Latina and Latino preachers face as we seek a theology to inform the *púlpito*: that theology must be ours without ceasing to be universal. Unfortunately, what passes

---

19 Timothy Tseng, foreword in *Conversations,* ii.
20 Kenyatta R. Gilbert, *A Pursued Justice: Black Preaching from the Great Migration to Civil Rights* (Waco, TX: Baylor University Press, 2016), x.

for universality often is little more than the perspective of the majority, or of those in power, imposed on the rest."[21]

Moreover, Native American or First Nations people also experience the watchful eye of theological suspicion and are expected to follow the theology of the majority. Richard Twiss, in his book *Rescuing the Gospel from the Cowboys,* observes: "For us First Nations people, following Creator-Jesus within our Indigenous cultural ways without submitting to the hegemonic cultural assumptions of today's conservative evangelicals is tough."[22] He continues: "Ignorance, suspicion and fear of Native ways run deep in the soul of the American church. ... Because we suffer so deeply, the entire church and nation does too!"[23]

For all ethnic minorities, the sentiment is that one is expected to give up one's ethnicity and culture and adopt a white, Western, North American perspective. This same ethos pervades North American evangelical theology and evangelical congregations. In light of such theological tensions among races and ethnicities, ethnic minority pastors, preachers, theologians, homileticians, and others must do the work of defining a theology that communicates to their culture.

To begin the process of defining ANA theologies, then, we must consult the rich and diverse experiences of ANA Christians and theologians in both written and oral forms. Our experiences define how we understand God and the world. ANA leading voices like DJ Chuang, the director of the L2 Foundation, a leadership and legacy organization devoted to Asian Americans, believes that many ANA scholars adhere to the belief that there are many ANA theologies and not one universal belief system.[24] For instance, Amos Yong points out:

---

21   Justo L. González, "Issues at the Púlpito," in *Púlpito: An Introduction to Hispanic Preaching,* by Justo L. Gonzalez and Pablo A. Jiménez (Nashville: Abingdon, 2005), 21.

22   Richard Twiss, *Rescuing the Gospel from the Cowboys: A Native American Expression of the Jesus Way* (Downers Grove, IL: InterVarsity, 2015), 17.

23   Twiss, *Rescuing the Gospel from the Cowboys,* 20.

24   Chuang, introduction in *Conversations,* vi.

Asian evangelical theologians also have at their disposal the wealth of theological resources from East and West to find a way between and beyond dichotomistic understandings of individualistic pietism and social liberationism, literalistic biblicism and hermeneutical relativism, and this-worldly versus other-worldly orientations. The fact is, actually, that there are multiple mediating trajectories in Asian evangelical theology, although they are less well known outside evangelical circles.[25]

The literature on ANA theology/theologies dissects the concept into a number of themes/categories. For our purposes, we might demarcate these into the following four topics: a theology of identity/image of God, a theology of marginalization, a quadrilateral theology, and a theology of incarnational duality.[26] Let's briefly explore these four themes, beginning with identity and the image of God.

IDENTITY AND THE IMAGE OF GOD

What tends to happen among proponents of Western theology is a flattening of racial/ethnic identities in favor of a universal Christian identity.[27] Some might argue that it's too complicated to consider all of the different variations of ethnicity and culture and how they impact theology. In other words, we should just preach Christ and the gospel and not concern ourselves with learning about people's unique and specific racial, ethnic, cultural, and other characteristics.[28] While first-generation immigrants tend to have a clearly defined ethnic identity from their native countries, second-generation and

---

25   Amos Yong, *The Future of Evangelical Theology*, 47.

26   Chuang, introduction in *Conversations*, vi–vii.

27   C. Eric Lincoln and Lawrence H. Mamiya, *The Black Church in the African American Experience* (Durham: Duke University Press, 1990), 12.

28   See Steve McAlpine, "How to be Culturally Intelligent in a Fractured Age," The Gospel Coalition (website), January 15, 2018, https://www.thegospelcoalition.org/reviews/preaching-with-cultural-intelligence/.

multigenerational ANAs struggle to determine whether they are Asian, Asian American, or Asian Canadian.

More specifically, most ANAs hold to an ethnic-specific identity like Korean American or Chinese Canadian rather than a broad racial identity such as Asian American or Asian Canadian. In the process of identity formation, one usually self-ascribes an identity, but there is also the influence of the label placed on them by others as one continuously forms his or her identity. For example, one might consider himself American, but members of the dominant culture always make him feel like an outsider who does not belong. Therefore, one vacillates between what one thinks of himself and the opinions of others of where he belongs in society. Put differently, it is "what they think your identity is" and "what you think your identity is."[29]

Paul Tokunaga, a third-generation Japanese American formerly involved in leadership with InterVarsity Christian Fellowship, illustrates this point effectively:

> On that 1–10 scale many of us live by, white folk were always a 10. I was convinced, as an Asian American, that the highest I could ever hit was a 7. I grew up in a predominantly white suburb in the San Francisco Bay area. It was clear to me, even as a child, that whites set the standards and I had to fit into their society if I was going to prosper, or even just survive. … I was embarrassed by my Japanese heritage. I wanted to be as white as I could. White was right. Japanese was not.[30]

As a result of this negative self-identity, the theology emerging among many ANAs is one of feeling unworthiness and non-acceptance from

---

29   Peter T. Cha, "Identity Formation in the Second-Generation Korean American Church," in *Conversations*, 5.

30   Paul Tokunaga, "Introduction: Learning Our Names," in *Following Jesus without Dishonoring Your Parents*, by Jeanette Yep, Peter Cha, Susan Cho, Van Riesen, Greg Jao, and Paul Tokunaga (Downers Grove, IL: InterVarsity, 1998), 9–10.

God. As Greg Jao, a Chinese American InterVarsity staff worker, experienced: "In a recent prayer meeting, I was startled as a quiet woman next to me burst out in prayer: 'God, we are not worthy to come to you! How can you stand us in your presence, O God? You are so holy and so good, but we are sinful, broken vessels. We do not understand why you accept our worship.' "[31] Many ANAs loathe themselves and carry a marred sense of self-esteem. Your very congregants may be struggling to love themselves as people made in the *imago Dei*.

One of the primary issues regarding the image of God pertains to ANAs' self-perception of having an inferior physical appearance. In her article, "13 Asians on Their Identity and the Struggle of Loving Their Eyes," Jessica Prois writes, "In America, there's a history of Asian eyes, racism and disenfranchisement. Propaganda signs at the time of Japanese American imprisonment during World War II or when the Chinese Exclusion Act was in force during the 19th and 20th centuries depicted characters with hyperbolized slanted eyes to dehumanize Asians. And these stereotypes persist today."[32] One Korean American woman that Prois interviewed responded: "Basically, all I wanted to do when I was younger was get old enough to get eyelid surgery, marry a white guy and change my last name immediately."[33]

While ANA women are generally perceived by whites and others to be exotic and attractive, ANA men, however, have historically been emasculated by whites and the wider media, being portrayed as nerdy, less masculine, socially inept, and therefore less attractive and desirable. As a case in point, Asian men are rarely lead characters in Hollywood productions, particularly in romantic roles. For instance, actor John Cho briefly played the lead character in a short-lived ABC romantic comedy, *Selfie*, starring as Henry Higgs who seeks to win the heart of Karen Gillan's character, Eliza Dooley. However, the

---

31   Greg Jao, "Spiritual Growth," in *Following Jesus*, 131.

32   Jessica Prois, "13 Asians on Identity and the Struggle of Loving Their Eyes," *Huffington Post*, updated May 30, 2018, https://www.huffingtonpost.com/entry/asian-american-eyes-photos_us_59f79448e4b0aec1467a3270.

33   Prois, "13 Asians on Identity."

network didn't renew the show for a second season, even though as one media writer explains: "No show more aptly captures the potent demographic forces that are reshaping America—and that have already transformed the millennial generation, the cohort currently in the process of inheriting the world."[34]

Historically, the United States has emasculated Asian men (particularly East Asians) through limiting their work opportunities to more "feminine" jobs, such as washing clothes or working in restaurants. One early American cartoon portrays a Chinese man wearing traditional Chinese garb and carrying a washboard. While some progress has been made over the centuries, Asian men and women are still portrayed by the media as inferior and "less than," which directly affects self-esteem and encourages self-hatred. In January 2017, comedian Steve Harvey showed a self-help book cover entitled: *How to Date a White Woman: A Practical Guide for Asian Men.* He asked the audience, "Excuse me, do you like Asian men?" and quickly responded himself with the words, "No. Thank you." The studio audience, comprising mostly women, erupted in hysterical laughter as a sign of agreement with Harvey's comment.[35] I do not write this to suggest that ANA women's self-images will always be confident or easier to define than ANA men's. ANA women have a host of concerns that have an impact on their identities and self-esteem, including pejorative notions of exoticism and fetishism, becoming slaves in the sex trafficking industry, and more.

How can Asians be made in the image of God when North American society often casts Asian men as less attractive and less welcome than people of other races? It's worth mentioning that living in a small New England town that is well over 90 percent Caucasian

---

34   Jeff Yang, "The TV Show 'Selfie' Is Now History—but It's Also the Future," January 8, 2015, https://qz.com/322898/the-tv-show-selfie-is-now-history-but-its-also-the-future/.

35   Maris Medina, "Asian-American Men Shouldn't Have to Defend Their Masculinity," *Diamondback,* November 16, 2017, http://www.dbknews.com/2017/11/16/asian-american-masculinity-stereotype-racism-feminization/.

and less than 2 percent Asian, I am often confronted with unwelcome stares or mean looks when I enter local mom-and-pop stores.[36] What hurts more is that when I drop off my kids at school, there have been many occasions when white students stare at my boys like they are in exhibits at the zoo. My third-generation Korean American children have been treated differently on their baseball all-star teams—relegated to hitting last or near the back of the batting order, playing only outfield positions, or even sitting on the bench most of the game—even though they are as talented as the white kids on their teams. And other subtle and overt forms of prejudice continue to manifest themselves even in the twenty-first century. I wish that ANAs could be treated as equals in the United States and that this wasn't my children's experience even as third-generation Americans. Yet, it's the insidious result of living in a fallen world where the majority rules. ANAs' self-images are complex and not a quick fix, yet there must be ways that preachers in ANA contexts can help our listeners develop a more positive self-image as Christians who happen to be ANAs. What do we need to understand before we can move forward?

A THEOLOGY OF MARGINALIZATION

Further complicating ANA theologies is the universal experience of marginalization for ANAs. One of the pioneering scholars on the Asian American theological scene (in the United States context) is Sang Hyun Lee, emeritus professor of systematic theology at Princeton Seminary. As with others mentioned throughout this book, Lee has experienced a lack of acceptance in white dominant American society. He writes:

> However long I stayed in this country, I seemed to remain a stranger, an alien. And this condition of being a stranger appeared to have two dimensions: the

---

36 "City Data," Beverly, Massachusetts (website), http://www.city-data.com/city/Beverly-Massachusetts.html.

experience of being in between two worlds, the Korean and the American, belonging to both in some ways, but not wholly belonging to either; and the sense that I as a non-white person might never be fully accepted by the majority of the dominant group in this country.[37]

As someone who does not fit the mainstream as a Korean immigrant, he interprets the Bible through a lens of being a stranger in a foreign land.

What Lee describes is a social phenomenon that Victor Turner referred to as liminality.[38] It is a feeling of being between two cultures while not fitting in to either one. It has also been called marginality or being on the outside looking in. The difference, according to Lee, is that marginality is a permanent form of liminality where entry is not allowed by the dominant culture. In response to marginality, Lee articulates two symbols of the Asian American historical experience that he labels pilgrimage and home.

The first image concerns that of the Christian experience as a form of pilgrimage where the Asian American Christian "is always ready to leave the present situation toward a God-promised goal."[39] He uses Abraham as a clear example of pilgrimage: "Abraham obeyed and left home when he was called, 'not knowing where he was to go,' and ... he and his family sojourned in the wilderness as 'strangers and exiles,' seeking the true 'homeland,' 'a better country,' 'the city whose builder and maker is God.' "[40] For Lee, the Christian Asian American experience is one of constant motion, where we cling to the hope of a better future in heaven as we deal with the daily grind

---

37 Sang Hyun Lee, "Pilgrimage and Home in the Wilderness of Marginality: Symbols and Context in Asian American Theology," in *Korean Americans and Their Religions,* ed. Ho-Youn Kwon, Kwang Chung Kim, and R. Stephen Warner, (University Park, PA: Pennsylvania State University Press, 2001), 55.

38 Victor Turner, *The Ritual Process: Structure and Anti-Structure* (Ithaca, NY: Cornell University Press, 1969), 94–203.

39 Lee, "Pilgrimage and Home," 61.

40 Lee, "Pilgrimage and Home," 61.

of our present earthly residence in the United States. It is a biblical understanding of the imminent future as hopeful to overcome the present state of liminality and marginality.

A second metaphor that Lee employs to describe the Asian American walk with Christ is "home." It is a place where Asian American pilgrims can find refuge and belonging. He writes: "What the symbol 'household of God' or 'home for the homeless' stands for receives a powerful expression in the Asian American church, which is one place in America where Chinese Americans, Japanese Americans, or Korean Americans feel like they are somebody."[41] In other words, home is a place where we can experience acceptance and healing from being outsiders in the dominant culture. This is one of the primary reasons why many ANAs continue to worship in English-speaking churches that are predominantly Asian in their demographics. It's the only place where they don't have to explain themselves or apologize in some manner for being themselves. Moreover, Lee observes: "Asian American theology in the context of marginality, in short, is an invitation for all to meet in the margins as fellow strangers and to stand by each other in solidarity as they join in God's own joyous struggle to build the household of God, where all of God's creation can come and be at home."[42]

A QUADRILATERAL THEOLOGY

In *Double Particularity: Karl Barth, Contextuality, and Asian American Theology*, Daniel Lee observes that there have been three traditional methods for understanding ANA theology: "the cultural, marginality, and postcolonial approaches."[43] Adding to these methods, Lee offers his own "constructive proposal, the Asian American Quadrilateral (AAQ) [which] represents a new way of defining the context as the intersection and the interaction of four layers: Asian heritage,

---

41   Lee, "Pilgrimage and Home," 65.
42   Lee, "Pilgrimage and Home," 69.
43   Lee, *Double Particularity*, 5.

migration experience, American culture, and racialization."[44] Lee's four-part sequence and the other ANA theological methods mentioned above are helpful but lack theological integration. While it is essential for a contextual theology to consider Asian cultures, migration, American society, and racialization, an anchoring theological doctrine or concept would ground the conversation more closely in theology. That is why I would like to suggest a theological model of incarnational duality.

TOWARD AN ANA THEOLOGY
OF INCARNATIONAL DUALITY

What constitutes the doctrinal core of evangelical Christianity? Put simply, Christianity distinguishes itself from all other world religions in its teaching on the incarnation of Jesus Christ, his perfect and sacrificial life, his death, his burial, his resurrection, his ascension, and his impending return. In articulating a contextualized ANA theology, I would like to draw on the dual nature of Christ: his divinity and humanity.[45] I will attempt now to put flesh on this idea of an incarnational duality. The concept of the dual nature of Christ sheds light on the dual nature of ANAs who are neither Asian nor North American, but rather *both* Asian *and* North American. In this final section on ANA theology, I will entertain how Christ's divinity and humanity form a helpful analogy to understand ANA theology and define what a hybrid ANA theology might look like.

Remembering Chalcedon

A contentious discussion among early church fathers ensued regarding how Jesus could be God and human at the same time in the same person. This led to the Council of Chalcedon in the fifth century (AD 451), which underscored the importance that "Christ is true God

---

44   Lee, *Double Particularity,* 5.
45   Thanks to Adonis Vidu at Gordon-Conwell Theological Seminary for sharing this valuable observation and insight.

and true man united in one person, the person of the Son of God in the Trinity."[46] Chalcedon clarified the dual nature of Jesus being truly God and truly man. Four affirmations arose out of this debate: (1) Jesus is fully divine; (2) Jesus is fully human; (3) the two natures are distinct; and (4) the two natures are completely united in one.[47] The Chalcedonian Creed can be summarized as:

> One and the same Christ, Son, Lord, only begotten, acknowledged in two natures that undergo no confusion, no change, no division, no separation; at no point was the difference between the natures abolished because of the union, but rather the property of both natures is preserved and comes together into a single person and a single hypostasis.[48]

How does the Chalcedonian Creed translate into the ANA experience? The ANA preacher or the preacher to ANA listeners must determine how Jesus' dual nature relates to the ANA person. Using points 1, 2, and 4 above, we can say that (1) ANAs are fully Asian; (2) ANAs are fully North American; and (4) the two natures are fully united in one person. The third part of Chalcedonian Christology is where our analogy breaks down. We cannot say that the two natures (Asian and North American) are distinct from each other. In fact, the true tension for ANAs is that they do not belong to either distinct group; yet, at the same time, they embody both groups to varying degrees.

Before unpacking these three similarities between a biblical Christology and ANA theology, let us say a few more things about

---

46   See "Creed of Chalcedon," Covenant of Grace Reformed Church, Accessed November 4, 2019, http://www.reformedspokane.org/Doctrine_pages/Christian%20 Doctrine%20pages/Eccumenical%20Creeds/Creed%20of%20Chalcedon.html.

47   "The Four Affirmations of Biblical Christology," Child of God's Grace, October 2, 2013, https://childofgodsgrace.wordpress.com/2013/10/02/ the-four-affirmations-of-biblical-christology/.

48   See John Anthony McGuckin, *The Path of Christianity: The First Thousand Years* (Downers Grove, IL: InterVarsity, 2017), 562.

the incarnation. Scripture includes numerous verses that clarify the meaning of the incarnation of Christ. For example:

- "But he was pierced for our transgressions, he was crushed for our iniquities; the punishment that brought us peace was on him, and by his wounds we are healed." (Isa 53:5)
- "The virgin will conceive and give birth to a son, and they will call him Immanuel (which means 'God with us')." (Matt 1:23)
- "The Word became flesh and made his dwelling among us. We have seen his glory, the glory of the one and only Son, who came from the Father, full of grace and truth." (John 1:14)
- Jesus "was delivered over to death for our sins and was raised to life for our justification." (Rom 4:25)
- "The Son is the image of the invisible God, the firstborn over all creation." (Col 1:15)
- "For we do not have a high priest who is unable to empathize with our weaknesses, but we have one who has been tempted in every way, just as we are—yet he did not sin." (Heb 4:15)

These and other passages proclaim that Jesus is God in the flesh. Jesus is fully God and fully human. Paul testifies that Jesus, "being in very nature God … made himself nothing by taking the very nature of a servant, being made in human likeness" (Phil 2:6–7). Jesus also lived a perfect, sinless life. He received the penalty of death for our sins. He suffered and was crucified on our behalf. Jesus took our punishment so that we might be exonerated and justified for our sins and receive eternal life with him. He was buried in a tomb and, three days later, resurrected from the dead. He ascended and went to heaven, and we eagerly await his second coming. In other words, Jesus possesses fully two natures in one person.

On Being Asian

As we consider the dual reality of being Asian and North American, let's first ask what it means for an ANA person to be Asian. Depending on whether the ANA person was born and/or raised in Asia or in North America, one will identify more or less with Asian culture, heritage, and tradition. Family upbringing contributes heavily to this identity placement. Did the ANA person's parents retain Asian cuisine, cultural traditions like Confucianism, ancestry veneration, and filial piety, native languages such as Chinese, Japanese, Korean, or Tagalog, and pass these cultural expressions on to their children (in this case, the second generation)? How much do these second-, third-, fourth-, and fifth-generation ANAs embrace Asian culture and values or reject them, such as the importance of the family name, the family's/parents' wishes over the individual's desires, collectivism/group think, educational and professional achievement, marrying the "right" person who comes from the same ethnic background, respect and care for the elderly and aging parents, and others?

This determination of one's Asian-ness or ethnic identification with being Chinese, Japanese, Vietnamese, or Korean is made on a case-by-case basis. Even some who are born in the United States or Canada may identify with their ethnic heritage more than being American or Canadian. Some Korean Americans that I know call themselves Korean, speak Korean, listen to K-Pop, eat traditional Korean cuisine, adhere to Korean/Eastern/Confucian values, and do not identify much with being American or Canadian. With each passing generation, it was assumed by sociologists that the next generation would lose or discard its "original" culture.[49] However, this phenomenon doesn't always occur. Taking time to ask questions and listen to one's story will help the preacher understand where this ANA person is coming from in their ethnic and racial gravitation.

---

49   Lisa Lowe, "Heterogeneity, Hybridity, Multiplicity: Marking Asian American Differences," in *Asian American Studies: A Reader,* ed. Jean Yu-wen Shen Wu and Min Song (New Brunswick, NJ: Rutgers University Press, 2000), 425.

On Being American or Canadian

Next, we must articulate what it means for an ANA person to be American or Canadian. Similar to the question above, ANA persons, depending on their place of birth, citizenship, nationality, family backgrounds and experiences, church experiences, education, friendships, sports, community involvement, marginalization and feelings of liminality, and other factors will find affinity with American or Canadian culture more than Asian or specific ethnic values. Of course, being American or Canadian means different things to different people. Damien Cave, a *New York Times* reporter, did a study in 2014, trying to get answers to the question: "What does it mean to be American?" He got numerous responses ranging from following rules, loving neighbors, working hard, being protected by the law, being free, having access, realizing the American Dream, and more.[50] Many ANAs want the dominant culture to see them as being equally American or Canadian, as someone who is Caucasian American or Caucasian Canadian, since they also place value on freedom, individualism, democracy, rights, and other common Western/ North American philosophies. Even writing the phrase "Caucasian American" or "Caucasian Canadian" is strange because that's the norm in society. Being American or Canadian is equated with being Caucasian. When one is Caucasian in North America, one is expected to be American or Canadian unless proven wrong by one's accent or passport. The same luxury is not afforded to ethnic minorities, including ANAs. Asians are assumed to be foreign-born, speak a foreign language, and practice a foreign culture.

On Duality

Finally, we must unpack the theory of the dual natures and understand that these two natures are fully united in one person.

---

50   See Damien Cave, "Day 39: On Being American," *New York Times,* May 17, 2014, quoted at https://www.facinghistory.org/my-part-story/what-does-it-mean-be-american.

Connecting Asian with North American is oxymoronic. The cultures are vastly different. Similarly, connecting Asian with theology seems to be an oxymoron. And yet, what does it mean for a racially/ethnically Asian person to be both Asian and American/Canadian? The theological concept of dual natures or duality has been described by sociologists of religion and other scholars on race and ethnicity such as hybridity,[51] double consciousness,[52] hyphenated,[53] third-culture,[54] and more.[55]

We see this tension of duality perhaps most profoundly in biracial and multiracial persons. The combinations of interracial/interethnic marriages are endless. Are they Asian and white, black and white, Hispanic and white, Native American and Hispanic, Asian and black, etc.? A college friend who is biracial (white and black) struggled to make sense of her racial/ethnic identity. Another friend whose father was Chinese and whose mother was Korean also struggled to come to a clear sense of his own identity. Was he Chinese? Korean? American? All three? None of the above? Two out of the three?

On the Practice of Duality

As we preach to ANAs, certain theological tensions exist. A primary example in the ANA context to help us understand dual natures regards a guilt-based versus shame-based theology. Let's briefly look at an example of what duality looks like in preaching to ANAs. In *Beyond Colorblind: Redeeming Our Ethnic Journey*, Sarah Shin explains

---

51   Brian Bantum, *Redeeming Mulatto: A Theology of Race and Christian Hybridity* (Waco, TX: Baylor University Press, 2016).

52   W. E. B. Du Bois, *The Souls of Black Folk* (Minneapolis: Lerner, 2016).

53   Young Park, *The Life and Times of a Hyphenated American* (Lincoln, NE: iUniverse, 2006).

54   Dave Gibbons, *The Monkey and the Fish: Liquid Leadership for a Third-Culture Church* (Grand Rapids: Zondervan, 2009).

55   Amos Yong identifies several common themes borne out of the Asian immigrant experience: "theology in quest of, journey theology, diaspora theology, theology of hospitality, theology 'betwixt and between' (neither Asian nor American), theology of homelessness, theology of hybridity, theology at/over the boundary and so on." See Yong, *The Future of Evangelical Theology*, 91.

that "guilt is different from shame, as guilt is the awareness of wrong-doing that leads to conviction and repentance. Shame, on the other hand, is the sense that one is irreparably, irrevocably broken."[56] North Americans tend to operate out of a guilt-based theology. Guilt comes out of a moral sense of right and wrong behavior or thinking. When the Holy Spirit convicts a person of sin and wrongdoing, the sinner experiences a sense of guilt over his or her misbehavior and appropriately confesses the guilt and repents for the sin. While guilt and shame go hand in hand at times,[57] shame in Asian contexts deals less with behaviors and actions and addresses more deeply things one cannot change about oneself, which can cause feelings of remorse and rejection on account of one's identity, personhood, appearance, race or ethnicity, cultural and value differences from the majority culture, and more.[58]

Yes, guilt and shame can be two sides of the same coin. One can experience guilt and shame in the same moment or even flip from guilt to shame or vice versa at some point. But in our preaching, teaching, and counseling, we tend to deliver messages, give lectures, teach Bible studies, and engage in conversations from either a guilt-based or a shame-based theology. An example of the difference between guilt and shame might be that a high school senior doesn't feel guilt over not being accepted to one's first-choice college, but rather he or she might internalize a sense of shame.

Another Christian might feel guilty about her unwillingness to tithe 10 percent of her income to the church, but she may not internalize a sense of shame. Shame enters the picture once her lack of tithing becomes publicized to at least one other person. If the pastor or church administrator confronted the church member about her

---

56   Sarah Shin, *Beyond Colorblind: Redeeming Our Ethnic Journey* (Downers Grove, IL: InterVarsity, 2017), 55.

57   See Joseph Burgo, "The Difference between Guilt and Shame," *Psychology Today,* May 30, 2013, https://www.psychologytoday.com/us/blog/shame/201305/the-difference-between-guilt-and-shame.

58   Yong, *The Future of Evangelical Theology,* 91.

financial stewardship, she may experience shame. Perhaps we might say it this way: guilt is more internal while shame is internal often in conjunction with external forces like other people's knowledge, awareness, response, gossip, or action. How, then, does this relate to the theology of the preacher?

If you're preaching a sermon from Acts 5:1–11 on Ananias and Sapphira, a theology of guilt might say: "There's a story about a husband and wife who lied about their giving to the church. As a result of lying to the Holy Spirit, the husband died. Later, when confronted about her husband's situation, the wife also lied. She too died on the spot as well on account of her deceitfulness." The guilt-based preacher allows the Holy Spirit through this story to convict his listeners.

A theology of shame would tell the same story but add a personal or corporate touch that would identify with those from shame-based cultures. Someone might say: "How do you feel after hearing this story? Is there any part of this story that you resonate with? Are we grieving the Spirit in any way?" We might even unknowingly or subconsciously heap shame on our listeners by being more direct and accusatory by saying things like: "Some of you may feel a sense of shame because you haven't been truthful to the Lord or to the church about your income and what it means to give 10 percent of your tithe to God. Perhaps some of you feel shame because you have made pledges to give to our mission fund or building fund and have failed to make good on your promises." Therefore, a contextualized theology of duality attempts to put flesh on Jesus' incarnation for the various sheep in one's congregation. To neglect one's ethnicity, race, culture, theology, church experience, et cetera would lack incarnational ministry as exemplified by Jesus.

CONCLUSION

Growing up in a conservative Korean American Presbyterian church near Chicago, the impressionable young souls in our children's ministry and youth group heard countless sermons that were thickly laden with the molasses of shame. In many sermons, God became an unpleasant tyrant, a disappointed father, a cosmic killjoy, or even—in Amy Chua's terminology—a tiger dad. I often left the Sunday worship services wondering: (1) Why is God so mean? (2) How could God love me when I'm so disgusting? (3) Why do I feel so horrible about myself so much of the time when I come to church? And on a lighter note, (4) Why is every application some version of "read your Bible and pray"?

In this chapter, I have identified some common approaches to theology from ANA scholars and have pointed toward a more integrated theology that intentionally accentuates both Asian and North American elements of a person. Some ANAs identify more with being Asian and others American or Canadian. The spectrum of ANAs is wide and varied.

The future of building a contextual ANA theology rests in the hands of all those who care deeply about the field. We want to appreciate the unique cultural diversity as expressed by God in his creation of different races, ethnicities, and cultures. We have our own voice in the theological conversation. I hope that you'll be able to spend time with your congregants and together articulate what it means to engage in ANA theological discourse and discovery.

To begin, I would suggest you consider more carefully and intentionally your theology and practice recognizing some of the theological elements that make your listeners Asian, American/Canadian, or both Asian and American/Canadian. One element of this theological duality concerns guilt versus shame. In appendix 1, you will find a worksheet that will help you in your weekly sermon and teaching preparation to work through some of the theological dualities faced by your listeners. Now that we have reworked hermeneutics and theology for ANA contexts, we will shift our focus to consider what ANA preaching looks like today.

QUESTIONS FOR REFLECTION
AND DISCUSSION

1. What are your congregants' views on God as a heavenly Father? Some ANAs have experienced difficult and strained relationships with their earthly fathers.

2. What are your congregants' views on Jesus' specific teachings that contradict Asian and North American values?

3. How does the Holy Spirit guide and inform ANA Christians today? What questions or reservations do ANA listeners have about the person and role of the Holy Spirit in their lives?

4. What attributes of God are held positively and negatively?

5. What isms are represented in your church (e.g., pluralism, syncretism, relativism, ecumenism, etc.), and how do they manifest themselves in congregational life?

6. What are the primary identities in your church (e.g., ethnic, racial, Christian, gender, occupational, economic, educational, generational, etc.)?

7. Is your congregation an honor culture, shame culture, both, or neither? How does this view influence their relationship with God?

8. What particular theological issues are most salient in your congregation? How do you address these topics?

CHAPTER FOUR

Daniel L. Wong

ASIAN NORTH AMERICAN PREACHING TODAY

Because I come from a Chinese American background, it is so natural that these would be the stories, dilemmas, and contexts that I share. This heightens the trust relationship between preacher and people, preacher and God's word, and provides strong bonds between God's word, the preacher, and the people. There's something special about speaking of what's familiar and common. Some of my sermons that people tell me they remember have to do with when I've shared about my mom's death, experiences of intercultural misses and awkwardness, of racism or put-downs, of shared jokes or recognition of experiences that we've had in common. ... It makes credible what we preach, because we show we understand the lives that we Asian Americans live in North America.

—Donna Dong, multiethnic ministry director,
InterVarsity Christian Fellowship of Canada

As we consider the ANA preaching scene today, we might use the metaphor of ice cream. If you took a blind taste test of an individual bowl of ice cream, you would be able to distinguish the unique taste of chocolate, strawberry, butter pecan, or a number of delectable flavors. It would be based on your past experience of tasting that flavor.

What is the "flavor" of ANA preaching? If we tasted an ANA sermon, could we immediately distinguish it from other flavors and voices?

We shouldn't be content with Russell Yee's assertion that there are "no particular Asian American … styles of preaching."[1] While it is true that ANA preachers have often preached generic sermons based on homiletic models learned in white North American seminaries, there are enough particularities of ANA preaching, preachers, and listeners that make it a vital area of study.[2] In this chapter, the goal is to orient you toward the current landscape of ANA preaching. We will take a short flight over the land of ANA homiletics and provide a bird's-eye view of the type of preaching that takes place in ANA congregations today. I know of no better way to begin to explore this than to share with you my own history as an ANA and an ANA preacher and draw out some lessons I've learned along the way.

MY JOURNEY AS AN ANA PREACHER

My earliest memory of hearing preaching was at the Chinese Cumberland Presbyterian Church in San Francisco's Chinatown. As a child, I vividly recall seeing two people at the pulpit: one speaking in Cantonese Chinese, which I did not understand, and the other interpreting the message into English with such a strong Chinese accent that I didn't understand him either. I was content to draw pictures on the bulletin.

In high school, my brother began attending a Chinese church in Oakland where we lived. It was different than the previous church and was composed of mainly American-born Chinese like me. There, I was impressed by the ministry and preaching of Reverend Alvin Louie. Due to his influence, I went to Moody Bible Institute. During

---

1   Russell Yee, "The Search for Asian American Worship," in *Chinese Around the World*, vol. 185 (Hong Kong: Chinese Coordination Centre for World Evangelization, 2004), 85. Also reprinted in *Asian American Christianity Reader*, ed. Viji Nakka-Cammauf and Timothy Tseng (Morrisville, NC: Lulu, 2009), 139–46.

2   See Matthew D. Kim, *Preaching to Second Generation Korean Americans: Towards a Possible Selves Contextual Homiletic* (New York: Peter Lang, 2007), 1.

my first year at Moody, I came back home and Reverend Louie asked me to share a message with the high school group. That was my first sermon, and my first sermon in an ANA context.

After graduating from Moody with a BA in foreign missions, I continued my education at Dallas Theological Seminary. I took the last preaching course Haddon Robinson taught there before he headed to Denver Seminary. That class introduced me to expository preaching, and I was sold. I also took a course on effective pulpit delivery from John Reed in which I preached a first-person narrative sermon. While in school, I was able to preach on occasion at our local church, the Chinese Chapel at First Baptist Church, Dallas, a mainly American-born Chinese congregation.

From 1982–1986, I was a full-time English ministry pastor at the Toronto Chinese Baptist Church. When the church expanded to two locations, I moved to the Scarborough Chinese Baptist Church and was there from 1986–2000. This involved regular preaching for an English-language congregation. During that time, and since becoming a full-time professor in 2000, I've accepted invitations to guest preach at various ANA congregations. These have been mostly English congregations in Chinese churches, but I've also gone to Korean churches, Vietnamese churches, Filipino churches, multicultural churches, and predominantly white Canadian churches. The guest speaking I've done in the United States has been mainly in English congregations in Chinese churches.

My advanced study in preaching has enriched my journey as an ANA preacher. From 1985–1989, I studied for a DMin at Trinity Evangelical Divinity School. There I was affirmed in my preaching gifts and deepened my expository preaching. My final project was called "The Use of a Sermon Feedback Group to Develop Application in Preaching," which combined my preaching with an adult Sunday school class following the sermon with a co-teacher. I also did an advanced academic study of preaching through the Toronto School of Theology, beginning with a church sabbatical from fall 1993 to the winter of 1994. I took six courses during that time, mostly on preaching, but also on the sociology of ethnicity and Canadian immigration history through the graduate program at the University of Toronto. Through this study, I broadened my understanding of preaching and was exposed to other ways of presenting sermons, especially through my involvement with the Academy of Homiletics.

There have been a number of lessons I have learned on this journey, first as an ANA preacher and now also as a teacher of preachers at Tyndale University. The first lesson is to "preach the word" (2 Tim 4:2). An important measurement of any sermon is whether the word of God was preached. Was there biblical content? Of course, the word needs to be communicated in a relevant and appropriate fashion. Often, though, the audience is easily impressed by an experience or story that can "preach," but unless the sermon is anchored in Scripture, it will fall on hard ground and not penetrate lives.

The second lesson is to contextualize for the congregation. When I was a full-time pastor, we worked with other pastors to discuss the direction and needs of the church and the English-language congregation. We planned preaching around these needs and where we sensed God was leading us. When guest preaching, I inquire of the pastor and/or leaders to help me settle on my main emphasis, such as the theme of the year and direction of the church. I often explore the church's website and listen to a sermon or two. I recall when there was a testimony/sharing time in the worship service and one father thanked the church for their support when his son committed suicide. I wished I was aware of this earlier. It would have given me more sensitivity to the congregation's feelings. One time I changed the topic and Scripture of a sermon once I observed and heard a congregation. We need sensitivity to the congregation and the Holy Spirit to make appropriate changes.

The third lesson is to make sure the sermon is not about me. I have a sensitive ego, or you could call it a pastoral heart. I get bothered when people fall asleep during the worship service and when

I preach. I have almost called people out who are watching a video while I preach. To do that would say more about me than them. When I guest speak, I can point these things out to the leaders after. They are already aware, no doubt. I need to pray and extend love and acceptance to the congregation. One time a couple was "fishing" during the sermon (bobbing their heads as they slept). I almost laughed but didn't say anything. Afterward, they came up to me and apologized, saying they had had to work late at a restaurant. I am glad they could even come to church that morning. There may be deeper issues involved too. People who are on their phones and not following the sermon may have a cell phone addiction. Of course, I need to see if my sermon is engaging and not assume that the congregation is struggling for other reasons but, at the same time, extend grace to those in the pews. As well, it can be tempting to use too many personal illustrations. Usually one illustration about myself is sufficient.

The fourth lesson is to keep growing as a preacher. We have focused on finding our voice in this book. Most of us have a default "voice," a bread and butter approach for which we are known. However, it is important to broaden that voice. Seek others who can give you honest feedback about your preaching. Get coaching and mentoring from an ANA pastor from whom you want to learn. I wish I had availed myself of that more. Essentially, I had no non-white teachers of preaching in all my homiletical education. Now there are ANAs who can teach and mentor ANA pastors.

To develop my voice, I have taken vocal lessons in the past and explored various genres of music. I have sung in choirs. When I almost lost my voice, I consulted a speech therapist (this ended up being due to allergies). Growth in our voices means we have something to preach that comes out of our own experience with God and our encounter with the word and Holy Spirit. "We preach and minister out of the overflow," I have heard it said. I listen to a litany of other preachers, seeking to hear their voice and how that voice can speak to me and what I can learn. I may be an experienced preacher, but it doesn't mean I am an accomplished one. There is always room to grow.

"Finding your voice and inspiring others to find theirs" is Steven R. Covey's advice in *The 8th Habit: From Effectiveness to Greatness.*[3] I have found my preaching voice and am constantly refining it with God's help. Through teaching, coaching, and mentoring students and pastors, I desire to inspire and equip them to find their voice. This book is part of that encouragement and inspiration.

In the next section, I want to further explore the voice of ANA preaching by focusing on three areas of exegesis that require ANA preachers' attention—the text, the congregation, and the preacher. Then I will name some common current practices of preaching in ANA contexts and discuss how preaching relates to the rest of worship in the ANA context.

EXEGETING THE TEXT FOR ANA PREACHING

Stephen Farris claims that when preparing to give a sermon, it is important for preachers to exegete the text, the situation, and themselves.[4] Just like preachers in other cultural contexts, the ANA preacher begins with understanding the text.

Since preaching is based on the Bible, the preacher needs to do spadework in the Scripture as the backbone for the sermon. ANA preachers are not exempt from this important task. Most evangelical preachers aim to find the "original" meaning of the text as the initial goal of exegesis. They use interpretive tools such as lexicons, concordances, word study books, and commentaries as companions for this work, whether in paper format or digital, using programs like Logos Bible Software.

3　Stephen R. Covey, *The 8th Habit: From Effectiveness to Greatness* (Stephen R. Covey, 2004).

4　Stephen Farris, *Preaching That Matters: The Bible and Our Lives* (Louisville: Westminster John Knox, 1998), 30–43.

As Matthew discussed in chapter 2, the preacher from an ANA background may not come up with the same interpretive results as those from African American, Hispanic American, or other backgrounds. Although the main interpretation will basically be the same, when thinking about how to communicate it, ANA preachers will take into account the cultural beliefs, values, and experiences of their ANA listeners. Looking through ANA eyes involves being attuned to nuances that will provide a more relevant and deeper understanding of Scripture for ANAs. As you read our sample sermons in appendix 2, take note of the ways that we have tried to anticipate our listeners' assumptions, conflicts, and questions about the Scripture passage.

Much of exegesis consists of asking questions. What are the parallels between the Bible and our context? What are the differences? This provides clues for the application to the congregation, and in that sense, it is difficult to draw a neat line between exegeting the text and exegeting the congregation. For example, honoring your parents is a prominent concept in Scripture. It is one of the Ten Commandments (Exod 20:10; Deut 5:16) and also a bedrock of Asian culture, as discussed in chapter 1. In an ANA context, we must ask, for example, how this biblical principle applies when a young person wants to be baptized and her parents disagree with this decision. Or what if the child wants to follow God's leading into a ministry calling and his parents are not supportive? To exegete the text in an ANA context involves asking informed questions that reflect the sociocultural milieu of ANA hearers.

Even though we cannot help but think about how to apply the text as we're doing our exegesis, we must always remember that faithfulness to the text is the aim for biblical preachers, including ANA preachers. We dig deep into the Scripture to understand its original meaning. We must have confidence that we have grasped what the text meant to its original audience before we can fully turn our attention to exegeting the congregation.

EXEGETING THE ANA CONGREGATION

Before I comment on what it means to exegete a congregation, it's important to lay out the frameworks for ANA congregations that exist in various church structures. Benjamin C. Shin and Sheryl Takagi Silzer have done the heavy lifting for us in naming different ANA church models in their book *Tapestry of Grace: Untangling the Cultural Complexities in Asian American Life and Ministry*.[5]

Denominationally, there is a spectrum in the Asian churches in North America. Korean churches are predominantly Presbyterian in background due to missionaries such as Horace Underwood who brought the gospel to Korea in the early 1900s.[6] Among the Chinese, there are many Baptist churches (for example, Southern Baptist, American Baptist, independent Baptist), which have a congregational form of church government. Regardless of denominational affiliation, ANA ecclesial models tend to have an explicit or implicit top-down organizational structure that underscores the parent-to-child relationship among the first and second generations in many Asian churches. Often the first generation maintains authority and dictates to the younger generations because of their "experience" as Christian leaders.

The most common ANA congregation attends an English worship service that is part of an ethnically Asian church. Both Matthew and I have served and preached regularly in these settings. English services arise when a specific ethnic group aims to reach people using its own language. A group gathers and develops into a church along the patterns of immigration. In time, children are born to the first generation. A children's program develops, then a youth ministry, and finally adult ministry. Along the way, an English service begins for children, youth, and then adults. Sometimes an interpreter aids

---

5   Benjamin C. Shin and Sheryl Takagi Silzer, *Tapestry of Grace: Untangling the Cultural Complexities in Asian American Life and Ministry* (Eugene, OR: Wipf & Stock, 2016).

6   Horace G. Underwood, *The Call of Korea: Political, Social, Religious* (New York: Revell, 1908).

the transition before an all-English service emerges. The English-speaking youth ministry takes time to develop, so it is usually the smaller of the two congregations. Over time, however, the English congregation can outgrow the original congregation due to locale and immigration patterns. The congregation might become more mixed with non-Asians by virtue of intermarriage and as non-Asian friends of the established congregation join. Often parents and leaders born overseas attend. Even some who want to learn English come to these church services. How diverse or homogeneous an ANA congregation is will in many ways dictate how much additional contextualization needs to happen in the sermon. One example of this diversity is the Boston Chinese Evangelical Church with American-born Chinese Steven Chin serving as the senior pastor.

One challenge faced by an ANA congregation nested within an immigrant church is the phenomenon of second-generation Christians.[7] Quite commonly, the first-generation immigrant Christian parents bear children who are raised in church. Of course, this is not unique among ethnic churches. More often than not, most of the English congregation would fit the category of second-generation Christians. Among second-generation Christians, there may be familiarity with the Bible but a lack of application of known truths. The concern is that the second generation is susceptible to "borrowed faith," in which the children do not accept Christ but faith is thrust upon them by their parents. In some cases, the second generation assumes that they are Christians by virtue of "living at church" and spending so much time there. All the while, they have never consciously put their faith in Jesus. Thus, Christianity becomes inauthentic and listening to sermons is just one more church routine.

The second ANA congregation type is the independent ANA congregation. This comes about when a maturing congregation of an ethnic church senses its need to branch out on its own. While not

---

7   Gordon T. Smith discusses this in *Beginning Well: Christian Conversion & Authentic Transformation* (Downers Grove, IL: InterVarsity, 2001), 207–18.

sacrificing their own English congregation, they plant an all English-speaking congregation. Other times pastors and members launch out on their own without the support of the ethnic immigrant church's blessing. This can lead to bitter feelings, misunderstandings, and accusations. The immigrant leaders may want to preserve the family bond under one roof of a church. Many of these church plants are attempts to stem the "silent exodus" of young people leaving ethnic churches.[8]

Within these two main types of ANA churches, there are a variety of different styles. One example of a church that started out as an independent ANA congregation but has evolved into something different is Evergreen Baptist Church of Los Angeles. Ken Fong, a third-generation American-born Chinese, founded Evergreen LA in an attempt to reach Americanized Asians. He addresses how to do this in his book *Pursuing the Pearl: A Comprehensive Resource for Multi-Asian Ministry.*[9] While Evergreen LA started as an ANA church, it has evolved over the years to have a broader multiethnic appeal. Fong has since retired, and the current senior pastor is Jason Ashimoto. Fong currently serves as an affiliate assistant professor of Asian American church studies at Fuller Theological Seminary, continuing to teach and preach at various venues. One of the ways that Fong has attempted to reach ANA listeners is to articulate shared experiences of ANAs, such as feeling shame as Asian people living in the United States and how this internalization has an impact on one's spiritual development and relationship with God.

DJ Chuang has called churches like Evergreen LA "next-gen multi-Asian churches." He describes this grouping as "autonomous English-speaking churches that are intentionally or incidentally serving next generation Asian Americans and multiracials, typically at

---

8   See the discussion in chapter 1.
9   Ken Uyeda Fong, *Pursuing the Pearl: A Comprehensive Resource for Multi-Asian Ministry* (Valley Forge, PA: Judson, 1999).

least 20% Asian."[10] Generally, these churches are small in size with a large proportion of ANAs. They are often younger in age than some of the English ministries within Asian churches. Many in the congregation may have migrated from an ethnic church, so they come with mixed feelings about culture and their place in society. A number of ethnically mixed marriages are usually evident in such congregations.

Other churches even designate "Asian American" in their name, providing racial identity and focus. One example is the Asian American Baptist Church in the Dallas area. The church's mission is "Renewing Asian Americans to be passionate followers of Christ."[11] Another example is the Marin Asian Community Church in the San Francisco Bay Area. It describes itself as "one of very few churches in Marin County with a special focus on ministering to English-speaking Asians. However, we gladly and warmly welcome individuals of any background. ... The goal of MACC is to be an effective witness to the community of Marin, the Bay Area, and to the rest of the world."[12]

Since ANA congregations exhibit such extensive diversity, how could we possibly exegete them? Of course, each congregation is different, but a number of general cultural considerations warrant our attention. First, there is generational identity. Does the congregation include ANAs in the first generation, 1.5 generation (in between the first and second), second generation, third generation, and so on? Do the people in the congregation subscribe more to North American cultural values, or have they retained, to a greater degree, the cultural values of their Asian ancestors? When do the two come into tension, and how might your preaching speak to that tension?

---

10   See https://djchuang.com/multiasian. Chuang expands on this concept in MultiAsian.Church: A Future for Asian Americans in a Multiethnic World (CreateSpace, 2016).

11   See Asian American Baptist Church, Accessed November 4, 2019, http://www.aabcdallas.org/.

12   See Marin Asian Community Church, Accessed November 4, 2019, http://marinchurch.org/about/.

Second, to what extent does the congregation synthesize Asian religions with Christianity? Are they still holding on to Asian religious practices? Are there ways in which your preaching should challenge that synthesis?

Third, which Asian ethnic groups are represented in the congregation? Are there people of Chinese ancestry, Japanese, Korean, Filipino, Indian, Vietnamese, or mixed races/ethnicities? Are there cultural realities that you need to be sensitive to in order to reach these people?

Fourth, education and occupation matter greatly in Asian contexts. But as we are aware, not all Asians are college graduates and work in professional careers. How can you preach in a way that connects with the range of education and experience that you find in your congregation?

These are not the only considerations. There are also some differences between the American and Canadian contexts. Ministry is further developed in the United States; there are more churches and more English congregations. In Canada, people think less about "Asian North American" as a category. Even the idea of "Asian Canadian" is foreign. Canada has multiculturalism built into its fabric and outlook, so more people identify with their specific ethnic group than a broad category like Asian.

ANA congregations are not uniform. They vary depending on size, history, denomination, ethnicities, generations, occupations, number of children, and other factors. As we preach to ANA listeners, it's necessary that we spend extra time asking the right interpretive questions as well as determining the appropriate illustrations and applications for who's listening. We will provide a bit more guidance on this in chapter 5.

EXEGETING THE PREACHER
IN THE ANA CONGREGATION

Preaching is impacted by the perspective and life experience of the preacher. It is necessary, therefore, for the preacher to carry out an "exegesis of the self."[13] Matthew calls this "exegeting the preacher."[14] This form of exegesis consists of examining ourselves in light of our personal journey. This may be the most difficult type of exegesis for all preachers, including ANA preachers. Inward exploration is not always easy. In a course at Tyndale University called "The Christian Life and Discipleship," I would often warn the students in the first class that the course would take them through a challenging journey. They would have to face themselves and look inward, which can be difficult. In fact, we often see the bad sides when we explore our histories. We go on a journey deep into the darkness of our own selves but come out on the other side in the light of the grace of God.

The main reason preachers need to exegete themselves is so that they can first preach every sermon to themselves—the toughest person in the congregation to preach to. As Haddon Robinson helpfully defines, expository preaching is "the communication of a biblical concept, derived from and transmitted through a historical, grammatical, and literary study of a passage in its context, which the Holy Spirit first applies to the personality and experience of the preacher, then through the preacher applies to the hearer."[15] The preacher needs to model to the congregation an embodied sermon application, and it is imperative that this flow from a vibrant spiritual life. Too often the Scriptures turn into a tool for teaching and preaching without a reflection of personal enrichment and a means to encounter God. Preachers need to speak out of the overflow of their relationship with God. How much richer would the spiritual impact be when the words of life are lived and experienced?

An exercise that is particularly helpful when exegeting yourself is to journal about your life. Matthew develops this exercise in

---

13 Farris, *Preaching That Matters*, 35–38.

14 Matthew D. Kim, *Preaching with Cultural Intelligence: Understanding the People Who Hear Our Sermons* (Grand Rapids: Baker Academic, 2017), 45–64.

15 Haddon W. Robinson, *Biblical Preaching*, 3rd ed. (Grand Rapids: Baker Academic, 2014), 5.

Preaching with Cultural Intelligence.[16] There are two basic steps to this exercise: (1) creating a personal timeline of your life with significant events and people, and (2) writing journal entries about your experiences. These help you to understand your family's dysfunctions and your ethnic background, identify your cultural attitudes, and connect with your pain. It is an intentional opportunity to reflect, confess, give thanks, and learn from your experiences. In particular, ANA preachers should ask, "How have you been encouraged by your Asian culture and shamed by it? What has been your experience of living as an Asian person in North America?" Taking the time to consider the joys and pains of being bicultural results in empathy and compassion for others. If you do not take the time to understand and deal with your background, it can easily spill over into your preaching, life, and ministry in a negative way. You could end up preaching out of frustration and anger because you haven't dealt with your buried emotions.

One issue that particularly requires self-exegesis in an ethnic church is that of esteem when it comes to language ability. Pastors can seem like fish out of water when they have the same ethnic background as the majority of the congregation but are not able to speak that language fluently. It is challenging to minister in a church where the expectation is to speak the mother tongue, and the temptation for preachers is to feel inferior. As an example, I began serving as a pastor for the Toronto Chinese Baptist Church in 1982. I was recruited to serve as the pastor for the English congregation, but "English congregation" was a misnomer, as there were two church services at the time: a 9:30 bilingual service in English and Cantonese and an 11:00 Cantonese service. Due to the limited size of the facility, there was not enough room for an all-English service in the sanctuary. My preaching was translated sentence by sentence into Cantonese. Later, when the church expanded to an additional location, there were two separate services, English and Cantonese. Often the youth were

---

16   Kim, *Preaching with Cultural Intelligence*, 51–61.

more astute than me in understanding and conversing in Cantonese. Most were second-generation Canadian-born Chinese. In cases like this, and in all cases, preachers need to find their identity in Christ (2 Cor 5:17). In him is the source of approval and self-acceptance. Working through these issues of feeling inferior or out of place while serving in an ANA church is not easy.

To become adept at self-exegesis and to gain emotional and spiritual stability, ANA pastors need support from others who know and understand ANA churches. Pastors can find support from others who face similar issues. Sometimes it is someone in the same city or it could be a connection from your time in seminary. Even online connections can facilitate sharing and support of ANA ministries.

It is particularly important to access coaches and mentors for ANA ministries. Larger cities tend to have associations where ANAs who lead English ministries can gather. The English-Speaking Chinese Ministerial in Toronto, of which I am a part, has been meeting monthly for over thirty-five years.[17] Here, mutual topics are discussed, including cultural issues in the church relating to first-generation leadership and transitions in ministry. We regularly invite new ministry graduates. We have met at Tyndale Seminary to interface with current students about English ministry. Several experienced pastors have shared their experiences as well as a Chinese-speaking senior pastor who is supportive of English ministry. There is also a Korean English Ministerial in Toronto called the Pastors' Fellowship Network, and we have had some joint meetings to discuss mutual issues. The San Francisco Bay Area and Boston each have an Asian American ministerial association.

Ultimately, the task of pastoral self-exegesis cannot be performed alone. Peter Cha and Greg Yee note that "if ANA churches are to grow as healthy households of God, the task of raising and

---

17   English-Speaking Chinese Ministerial, http://www.escm.hhosts.net.

sustaining healthy pastors is key."[18] Both Matthew and I are committed to mentoring and supporting pastors in ANA congregations. It is particularly encouraging when congregations enlist experienced pastors to mentor their less experienced pastors. This is starting off on the right foot to provide support. When things get remedial, it is often too late.

In short, ANA preachers require self-exegesis to remain healthy and fruitful in ministry. My hope is that you'll make time to pray about and review your own walk with the Lord. If you reach out, you will find the necessary support and help.

CHARACTERISTICS OF ANA PREACHING

I will now cover specific characteristics that are common among preachers in ANA contexts or could be included more intentionally. ANA preaching should be contextual, intercultural, incarnational, Holy Spirit-led, transformational, narratival, and collaborative. As you read, consider this question: What practice(s) specific to an ANA context characterize your sermons? It may be one or more of these or something else.

Contextual

Preachers preach in the context of their congregation. All sermons should be congregation-specific. The apostle Paul drew from the cultural context of his audience when he preached to the Athenians in Acts 17:16–34. In this sermon, he referred to idols and Greek poets, and he applied the message specifically to his hearers.[19] This is in contrast to his speeches to predominantly Jewish audiences (Acts 22, 26), which are laced with Old Testament stories and characters.

---

18   Peter T. Cha and Greg J. Yee, "Forming 'Grace-Full' Pastors," in *Honoring the Generations: Learning with Asian North American Congregations,* ed. M. Sydney Park, Soong-Chan Rah, and Al Tizon (Valley Forge, PA: Judson, 2012), 97.

19   Daniel L. Wong, "Preaching in a Multicultural World," *Preaching: The Professional Journal for Preachers* 23:5 (March/April 2008): 13–16.

Matthew has written about how his preaching was transformed when he decided to design his sermons for the second-generation ANA teenage context:

> My sermons required a complete makeover. Not only did I need to preach from my life experiences as a bicultural Korean American, but also my sermons needed to be shaped in a way that my second-generation Korean-American listeners would understand and embrace. I started to use illustrations from my life experiences growing up as a bicultural Korean American and all of the pleasures and baggage that go along with being an Americanized Asian-American Christian. When I began to engage with my Korean and American DNA and my second-generation Korean-American teenage listeners, my preaching took a positive turn.[20]

Daniel K. Eng, who completed his DMin in Asian American Ministry at Talbot Seminary and is a PhD candidate at Cambridge University, similarly expresses his journey in contextual preaching: "I used to fear that contextualization would make someone who is not Asian American feel less comfortable with my sermons. However, I realized that there is such a shortage of Asian American contextual preaching that 'white-washing' my message would make me miss an opportunity to have a deep impact in my primary audience."[21]

Too often, ANA preachers aim to preach generically. Their sermons could be preached in any context without adjustment for a specific congregation, ethnicity, culture, or location. There are no ANA-specific illustrations or applications in their message. Haddon Robinson advocates for contextual preaching in his essay "Preaching to Everyone in

---

20   Matthew D. Kim, "Asian-American Preaching," in *The Art and Craft of Biblical Preaching: A Comprehensive Resource for Today's Communicators,* ed. Craig Brian Larson and Haddon Robinson (Grand Rapids: Zondervan, 2005), 203.

21   From Eng's response to Daniel L. Wong's questionnaire.

Particular: How to Scratch where People Niche." He brings poignant insight on the need to adjust to your audience: "Speaking to a broader audience requires a sacrifice from us. We give up our freedom to use certain types of humor, to call minority groups by names that make sense to us, to illustrate only from books and movies we find interesting, to speak only to people with our education and level of Christian commitment."[22] This sacrifice may feel constricting, but refusing to do it will hinder our ability to connect with our audience.

One of the ways that we can improve the contextualization of our sermons is to do some work in advance. For instance, when I am a guest speaker (usually in English-speaking ANA congregations), I inquire beforehand about the specifics of the congregation. I explore the website to find their vision, mission, and values. I will speak to the pastor to learn about recent sermon series and current events in the church's life. What is the age range of the congregation? In ANA congregations, the youngest age can be junior high or senior high. What is the majority age group? What is the ratio of women to men? What is the ethnic makeup? Answering all these questions beforehand will help preachers to speak specifically to the context of a congregation.

When you are the regular preacher, the message can be further shaped with the ANA context in mind. Even speaking to certain segments of listeners or using illustrations and applications that would be particularly pertinent can be exercised. Congregations that have a keen interest in sports might appreciate illustrations that point to Michael Chang and more recently Jeremy Lin as examples of ANA Christians living out their faith in the spotlight. We might also use examples from the work of ANA authors like Celeste Ng or Kevin Kwan, actors like John Cho, Sandra Oh, or Simu Liu, musicians like Ji-Hae Park or Yo-Yo Ma, fashion designers like Vera Wang, and even

---

22   Haddon W. Robinson, "Preaching to Everyone in Particular: How to Scratch Where People Niche," in *Making a Difference in Preaching*, ed. Scott M. Gibson (Grand Rapids: Baker, 2002), 118–28.

politicians like Andrew Yang. To connect with segments of the congregation, Ronald J. Allen created a grid to track how the illustrations and applications have intentionally connected.[23] The preacher can keep track of which illustrations primarily intersect with which segments of the audience over a month's time.

As congregation members sense that the preaching connects with them, they pay closer attention to the sermon. They are more likely to respond. Contextual preaching is a goal of any preacher who approaches ministry and preaching in an incarnational way.

Incarnational

Incarnational preaching is preaching that intersects with the lives of congregation members via relationships. It has an emphasis on heart-to-heart communication. Stephen and David Olford explain that "the incarnational approach to preaching calls for and encourages authentic preaching from the heart. Also, incarnational preaching should foster a concern to preach to the hearts of others."[24] Jesus Christ is the primary example of incarnation, becoming human to live among us relationally and sacrificing himself for us (John 1:14; Phil 2:1–11). For pastors, preaching that is incarnational emerges out of spending time with people, particularly during informal times.

This incarnational approach must be done intentionally by being among the people in their world. Although the church facility might be the world of the pastor, it is not the everyday world of the congregation members. Rather than spending so much time in the church office or building, the pastor would benefit by going off-site. Pastors can visit members in their homes, at work, at the coffee shop,

---

23   Ronald J. Allen, "The Social Function of Language in Preaching," in *Preaching as a Social Act: Theology and Practice,* ed. Arthur Van Seters (Nashville: Abingdon, 1988), 183.

24   Stephen F. Olford and David L. Olford, *Anointed Expository Preaching* (Nashville: B&H Academic, 2003), 209. A related concept is "identification," which I see as one way to pursue incarnational preaching by connecting with the life and experiences of the congregation. See Craig A. Loscalzo's *Preaching Sermons that Connect: Effective Communication through Identification* (Downers Grove, IL: InterVarsity, 1992).

and other places that the members identify with, as well as joining a family for significant events like their child's graduation, music recital, or softball game. For those of us who have mainly a theological education and less experience in the general working world (like me), this education is invaluable. Jonathan Hong connects this incarnational strategy to preaching by saying that when he prepares a sermon, he begins "by first understanding well whom it is that I am preaching to. This means that I make it an effort to spend time with and hear the joys and struggles of my congregants."[25]

To become more incarnational in our preaching, we should not be reluctant to share personally. Andy Stanley advises in his preaching book, *Communicating for a Change,* to begin the sermon with a section on "me" to connect with the congregation.[26] Although every sermon does not need to begin this way, the personal dimension is helpful to include somewhere in each sermon. While the sermon is not about the preacher, you can reveal something autobiographical to drive home a point. Among well-known ANA preachers, Eugene Cho and Francis Chan frequently refer to their cultural backgrounds in their speaking.[27]

There are cautions about this approach, however. There needs to be a healthy balance of sharing negative and positive experiences; be sure you are not always the hero or the heel. There can also be oversharing and taking up too much of the sermon with personal illustration. But without the personal dimension, there is too much distance from the congregation. It is particularly powerful in an ANA context when preachers are able to reveal where they have had to struggle to find resolution between cultural values and the gospel. Russell Yee,

---

25   Correspondence with Jonathan Hong, English Ministry pastor at Toronto Korean Presbyterian Church.

26   Andy Stanley and Lane Jones, *Communicating for a Change: Seven Keys to Irresistible Communication* (Portland, OR: Multnomah, 2006), 120–24.

27   Although Nate Lee has argued that Chan has a tendency to deprecate his cultural heritage, especially in front of predominantly white audiences; see Nate J. Lee, "Francis Chan's Ethnic Identity Journey," *NJL* (blog), July 14, 2014, http://natejlee.com/francis-chans-ethnic-identity-journey.

a preacher, worship leader, and songwriter, expresses this tension in his song "Never Not in Need of Grace." The first verse is as follows:

> I work really hard and hardly complain.
> I try not to show it when I'm in pain.
> I plan what I say, and keep to my space;
> But I'm never not in grace, no;
> I'm never not in need of grace.
> Please save my soul, not just my face,
> I'm never not in need of grace.[28]

We vividly hear the struggle as this ANA preacher yearns for grace against the backdrop of his shame-based cultural heritage.

Incarnational preaching highlights the connection of preacher to congregation by using illustrations and applications common to both. While this type of preaching emphasizes the similarities, intercultural preaching can identify the differences.

Intercultural

Preachers need intercultural skills if they want to communicate well in any congregation.[29] When any two people interact, some kind of intercultural encounter usually takes place. In preaching, you have one person speaking to many people of diverse cultures. While it seems like ANA congregations are homogeneous—a sea of black hair and almond-eyed individuals—there is a diversity of cultures in each one. The one-to-many dynamic brings more intercultural challenges than a one-to-one interaction and a greater need for sensitivity. It takes a lot of wisdom and experience to navigate this.

---

28   Russell Yee, "The Search for Asian American Worship."

29   Jared E. Alcántara, *Crossover Preaching: Intercultural-Improvisational Homiletics in Conversation with Gardner C. Taylor* (Downers Grove, IL: IVP Academic, 2015) 191–236; Daniel L. Wong, "An Intercultural Homiletic: Preaching Amidst Cultures," paper presented at the 39th Annual Meeting of the Academy of Homiletics, Memphis, Tennessee (2004): 308–16; and Kim, *Preaching with Cultural Intelligence.*

Intercultural skills help us to develop sensitivity to the "other," to the one who is different from us. This person may be someone from a different generation, or a refugee from a war-torn country who is struggling to adjust to a new country and the English language. Just like a missionary learns the language of the host country and about its culture, the intercultural preacher should make the effort to learn the culture and language of segments of the congregation. This is simply good pastoral practice.[30]

My mentor, Alvin Louie, promotes learning Chinese as an American-born Chinese himself.[31] While he dropped out of Chinese school during his youth, Louie elected to learn Cantonese and Mandarin formally to enhance his ministry. His perspective is that this language acquisition "helps build bridges in the ministry."[32] Of course, pastors need to advocate for the English congregation and not spend all their time learning Chinese, but having a sensitivity to language shows honor and respect for those who are often older in age and mature in the faith. I have tried to pick up Chinese in the context of the church and use it (always trying to maintain the proper dialect) with older members and leaders. My experience is that by "osmosis" the pastor picks up some understanding of the language. However, I have also embarked on formal and informal studies of both Cantonese and Mandarin Chinese. I hope to learn Korean in the near future.

Another intercultural pastoral practice involves eating food that originates from different cultures. Having meals that correspond to the various ethnic groups in your congregation can be fun. It is a catalyst for conversation. Once I went with a primarily Chinese group of leaders out to eat at a Korean restaurant with a Korean pastor during

---

30   A good resource for this is Dan Sheffield, *The Multicultural Leader: Developing a Catholic Personality,* 2nd ed. (Toronto: Clements Publishing, 2015).

31   Alvin Louie, "Should an ABC Pastor Study Chinese?," in *A Winning Combination: ABC/OBC: Understanding the Cultural Tensions in Chinese Churches* (Petaluma, CA: Chinese Christian Mission, 1986), 103–08.

32   Louie, "Should an ABC Pastor Study Chinese?," 104.

Lunar New Year. You could tell that they had not eaten Korean food before. This was a positive learning experience of another culture.

In sermons themselves, it is important to think about how to communicate effectively across the different cultures represented in your congregation. During my sermon that is reprinted in appendix 2, I referenced the "clay pots" in 2 Corinthians 4:7. Then I displayed a flower pot. It was ordinary, but it contained an expensive and exotic orchid. I then showed a rice bowl that is commonly used in Chinese restaurants and Asian homes. Ordinary bowls can contain expensive food. In the same way, we are ordinary but carry within us the extraordinary message of the gospel.

With the broadening of ANA churches to more people groups, the intercultural dimension of preaching becomes even more crucial. In these contexts, sensitivity in navigating cultures becomes a key trait for the preacher.

Holy Spirit-Led

In his book *Conformed to His Image*, Kenneth Boa draws a distinction between word-centered preaching and Spirit-centered preaching.[33] Word-centered preaching is preaching where the focus is on the text or texts of Scripture. While this often results in solid biblical teaching and good note-taking, preaching that touches the hearts and spirits of listeners requires a greater emphasis on the role of the Holy Spirit. This goes beyond the communication of information. In our preaching, we should long to mirror the apostle Paul: "My message and my preaching were not with wise and persuasive words, but with a demonstration of the Spirit's power" (1 Cor 2:4).

Greg Heisler develops the concept of Holy-Spirit-led preaching in *Spirit-Led Preaching: The Holy Spirit's Role in Sermon Preparation and Delivery.* According to Heisler, in sermon preparation, the Holy Spirit

---

33 I was introduced to the distinction of word-centered vs. Spirit-centered in Kenneth Boa's *Conformed to His Image: Biblical and Practical Approaches to Spiritual Formation* (Grand Rapids: Zondervan, 2001), 291–320.

should influence text selection, prayer and study, sermon development, and internalizing the text.[34] The delivery also must be done with the Spirit's empowerment.

When I teach preaching, I say that the longer one refrains from turning to commentaries, the better. It is better to do inductive work in the text and allow the Holy Spirit to speak to you. It is not that the Holy Spirit cannot use commentaries and other helps, but the interaction with the text as guided by the Holy Spirit is important for maintaining the openness to the Spirit that is necessary for Spirit-led preaching.

Prayer is intimately connected with the Holy Spirit and preaching. The whole process of sermon preparation should be saturated in prayer, or "prayer drenched."[35] Ajith Fernando says, "Sometimes when we are in the middle of preparing for an assignment, such as writing a sermon, God may prompt us to stop the preparation so as to prepare ourselves. When we sense this need, it would be wise to stop immediately and go to prayer."[36]

While many sermons in ANA churches could be classified as word-centered, some ANA preachers are highlighting the importance of prayer and a conscious dependence on the Holy Spirit in sermon preparation. Peter Cha writes about how he learned this growing up as an ANA pastor's son: "I grew up watching my father, a Korean pastor, spending much time in prayer before he preached each Sunday. His sermons were simple but powerful. As a young preacher, I learned from him that transformative preaching is ultimately the work of the Holy Spirit, so a preacher must pray fervently before and during one's preaching."[37]

---

34   Greg Heisler, *Spirit-Led Preaching: The Holy Spirit's Role in Sermon Preparation and Delivery* (Nashville: B&H Academic, 2007), 88–100. James Forbes earlier alerted preachers to the Holy Spirit's role in *The Holy Spirit & Preaching* (Nashville: Abingdon, 1989).

35   Daniel Fusco, "4 Practices to Stay Connected to the Power of the Holy Spirit," *Preaching Today*, July 2017, http://www.preachingtoday.com/skills/2017/july/preaching-in-power-of-holy-spirit.html.

36   Ajith Fernando, *Jesus Driven Ministry* (Wheaton, IL: Crossway, 2002), 43.

37   Correspondence with Peter Cha, professor of church, culture, and society at Trinity Evangelical Divinity School.

Many ANA preachers could learn a lot from churches with a Pentecostal background, which strive to be in tune with the Holy Spirit and prayer in all of ministry. I have appreciated the writing and ministry of Siang-Yang Tan, who brings out the role of the Holy Spirit and prayer for pastoral ministry. I met him in Toronto when he was teaching a Tyndale Seminary course called "Counseling and the Holy Spirit." I recommend his books, *Shepherding God's People*[38] and the cowritten *Disciplines of the Holy Spirit*,[39] which feature the role of the Spirit for ministry and life in general from an ANA perspective.

Transformational

God seeks change in people. One reason why we should prefer Spirit-centered preaching to word-centered preaching is that we know God wants to see people transform into the image of Christ. It is ultimately the work of the Holy Spirit, yet God is gracious in using the preacher in the process of transformation. The preacher is instrumental when congregation members explicitly or implicitly say, "What shall we do?" (Acts 2:37) or "What must I do to be saved?" (Acts 16:30). The preacher supplies the message to which the congregation responds.

Matthew's definition of expository preaching includes the purpose of transformation: "Expository preaching is communicating God's Word boldly, clearly, and tangibly for the purpose of life transformation in the preacher and in the listeners."[40] It is important to underscore that transformation is not just for the congregation; both the preacher and the listeners need to be transformed. As Ken Fong rightly notes, "To become a transformational preacher, you must be

---

38   Siang-Yang Tan, *Shepherding God's People: A Guide to Faithful and Fruitful Pastoral Ministry* (Grand Rapids: Baker Academic, 2019).

39   Siang-Yang Tan and Douglas H. Gregg, *Disciplines of the Holy Spirit: How to Connect to the Spirit's Power and Presence* (Grand Rapids: Zondervan, 1997).

40   Matthew D. Kim, "Interview," in *Models for Biblical Preaching: Expository Sermons from the Old Testament,* ed. Haddon W. Robinson and Patricia M. Batten (Grand Rapids: Baker Academic, 2014), 172.

transformed first."[41] The importance of remembering the preacher's own transformation was highlighted for me when I was consulting with an English ministry pastor of a Chinese church who was planning to preach a series on evangelism. He had each sermon laid out, but it seemed something was missing. I felt constrained to ask this preacher, "What are you doing to model evangelism?" The preacher was dumbstruck; he didn't know how to answer. He would need to apply his sermon himself—to be transformed himself—before he expected his congregation to do the same.

When you preach for transformation, you pray and strategize for changed lives. This means prayerfully planning the intended outcome of the sermon. Focus on how the congregation might apply the message as a whole and as individuals. Ask questions like: What is the purpose of my sermon? What does it set out to accomplish? What change am I seeking in my audience's thinking, being, or doing? It is particularly important in ANA contexts to consider both individual and corporate application. How does this sermon impact my listeners on their own, their immediate or nuclear family, and the entire church family? Application needs to be built into sermons with specific suggestions for carrying out the message.

Ajith Fernando writes about the impact of sermons: "Sermons should disturb, convict, and motivate to radical and costly obedience. I have wondered whether people's desired result from sermons is to enjoy themselves rather than to be changed into radical disciples who will turn the world upside down."[42] Christian disciples are indeed followers of Jesus Christ. To follow Christ includes applying sermons to lives and seeing life transformation personally. This includes the transformation of the preacher, individuals in the congregation, and the congregation as a whole.

---

41   Ken Fong, "Transformational Preaching," PowerPoint presentation from Transformational Preaching in Asian American Context course, Fuller Theological Seminary, Spring 2016.

42   Fernando, *Jesus Driven Ministry*, 23.

Narratival

In the past, the typical sermon had an outline that contained three points, usually beginning with the same letter of the alphabet. However, recent preaching has been characterized by narrative. There is a story element to sermons. This is particularly true of ANA preaching.

The reason for this shift is simple: people connect with stories. Peter Cha underscores the need for narrative in sermons: "Storytelling is a key vehicle through which I attempt to communicate some key themes of the biblical text. So as an Asian American preacher, I strive to grow as a story teller so that I can be more effective in preaching narrative passages and in using stories effectively as illustrations."[43] Paul Tokunaga advocates to "preach narratively because it connects with a relational culture."[44] Ken Fong recounts his journey toward a more narrative style of preaching: "Convinced that a story-telling style was the key to reaching the heart of Asian Americans, I dumped the outline inserts in 1987, and I quit trying to preach as if my professors were there each week. Instead, with fear and trembling, I began to tell the story that God has spoken to us through his Word and our personal histories."[45] God's story connects with our stories.

Some bemoan that narrative sermons lack content. Don't get me wrong: sermons need good content. There also needs to be progress and development in the sermon. Content is enhanced by how you present it. Explanation of the text should be included as well as illustration. Sections of Scripture that are more didactic, like the Epistles, may have more points and content, especially when they arise naturally from the biblical text.

---

43   Correspondence with Peter Cha.

44   Paul Tokunaga, *Invitation to Lead: Guidance for Emerging Asian American Leaders* (Downers Grove, IL: InterVarsity, 2003), 206.

45   Ken Uyeda Fong, *Pursuing the Pearl: A Comprehensive Resource for Multi-Asian Ministry* (Valley Forge, PA: Judson, 1999), 134.

Collaborative

Preaching is not an individual endeavor. It involves the Holy Spirit, as
mentioned above, as well as the congregation. Collaboration reflects
the body of Christ as each one contributes to the whole. The apostle
Paul makes this clear in 1 Corinthians 12. While only one person can
preach at a time, the sermon can express the collective contribution
of congregation members.

A key element of collaboration is prayer. There was a reciprocal
prayer relationship between the apostle Paul and his congregations.
Paul prayed for them and asked for prayer, particularly that the word
would go forth clearly and he would preach boldly (Eph 6:19–20; Phil
1:3–6; Col 4:2–6). John C. Maxwell recounts learning about prayer
partnership:

> On a Tuesday morning after I'd been at Skyline for
> about six weeks, I was reviewing the day's schedule
> when I saw an appointment scheduled for a person
> whose name I didn't recognize.
>
> "Who's Bill Klassen?" I asked.
>
> "He's your ten o'clock appointment," replied Barbara,
> my assistant.
>
> "I see that, but who is he? Is he in leadership?" I
> asked. I had spent the last few weeks focusing much
> of my attention on getting to know the leaders in the
> congregation.
>
> "No, he's not in leadership," said Barbara. "As a matter
> of fact, he doesn't even go to church at Skyline." Barbara
> could see that I wasn't happy. "He said he had to see
> you. He was very persistent," she added emphatically.
>
> "Well," I said, "give me about fifteen minutes with
> him, and if we're not done, interrupt us." My plan was
> to figure out what his agenda was, fix whatever problem

he had, kindly but quickly, and get on with the work I had to get done that day.

Bill turned out to be a gentleman of about sixty with hair white as snow. His face was gentle, almost radiant. … He began telling me about himself, how he had worked in construction in Canada and sold sailboats in Washington and southern California, and how he had worked for the Navigators ministry as a discipler.

"John," Bill said. "I believe God has called me—a layman—to disciple, encourage, and pray for pastors. And the reason I came here today was so that I could pray for you."

He wanted to pray for me? I thought. In all my years as a pastor, I've never had a layman pray for me. My own agenda began to melt away. I felt the Spirit of God crushing me, saying, "John, my agenda is more important than yours. Your life is not like a one-way street where you just minister to other people. There are people who want to minister to you. I am sending this layman to pray for you." [46]

ANA preachers should pray and seek intercessors who can pray for their ministry and preaching as well. It is easy for pastors to think of themselves as the ones who are always praying for others, but prayer ministry is reciprocal. When you ask how you can pray for someone, you also ask that person to pray for you. I often enlist people to regularly pray for me when I'm preaching. Recently, I was at a church, and a layperson asked how he could pray for me. I asked that he pray for

---

46 John C. Maxwell, *Partners in Prayer: Support and Strengthen Your Pastor and Church Leaders* (New York: Thomas Nelson, 1996), 2–3. See also C. Peter Wagner, *The Prayer Shield: How to Intercede for Pastors, Christian Leaders and Others on the Spiritual Frontlines,* rev. ed. (Glendale, CA: Regal, 2014). While some of Wagner's work has drawn controversy, this volume is straightforward and practical, developing an important area.

clarity and that the Spirit would empower my sermon. I had him pray for me, and I prayed for him right there before the worship service.

Collaboration in preaching also involves feed-in and feedback. "Feed-in" refers to discussing the sermon's topic and themes beforehand with others in the congregation. This can happen in person or over email; the preacher may send the sermon passage out in advance to church members to gauge what questions they have about it and what illustrations and applications they might suggest. Particularly in areas that the preacher is less familiar with, input is important. For the younger or unmarried preacher, this may be in the area of marriage and raising a family. Many ANA congregations have a learning time or Sunday school after the church service. In one congregation where I used to speak regularly, the hour after the service was devoted to discussing the sermon. I would provide discussion questions, and often the session would begin with feedback to me and questions for me to clarify. This was helpful. Honest and accurate feedback keeps the preacher on track and on target to connect with the congregation.[47]

THEMES AND TOPICS IN ANA PREACHING

In addition to the general characteristics of ANA preaching, there are also some Scripture themes that are particularly pertinent to ANA congregations. Like many evangelical preachers, those in ANA congregations often preach through Bible books or base their sermons on topics that are rooted in passages of Scripture. But if ANA preachers want to speak to the particular needs and concerns of their congregation, they should consider the cultural realities faced by ANAs.

One theme in Scripture that resonates sharply with ANA congregations is the relationship between law and grace. ANAs who may be caught up in an achievement mentality have an ongoing

---

47   Daniel L. Wong, "The Use of a Sermon Feedback Group to Develop Application in Preaching" (DMin thesis, Trinity Evangelical Divinity School, 1989). The focus of this project was developing the application of sermons particularly related to a co-taught Sunday school class on "How to Get More Out of a Sermon."

need to understand and experience grace. This makes Paul's Letter to the Galatians an especially good book for a sermon series in an ANA context.

Leadership is another core theme that ANA listeners need to hear about regularly, particularly the delicate dance of passing on leadership responsibilities from one generation to the next. Joshua is an important book that features a new leader taking on responsibility for the new generation. Likewise, Paul's letters to Timothy speak of the younger pastor, Timothy, leading the Ephesian church. I often encourage pastors preparing for ordination to read through the Pastoral Epistles with a view to character and pastoral responsibilities. In Paul Tokunaga's *Invitation to Lead: Guidance for Emerging Asian American Leaders,* he takes Moses and Esther as biblical paradigms for leadership in an ANA context. He observes, "Moses and Esther are role models for Asian Americans, not that they did everything right but because we can identify with much of what they encountered and wrestled with. More important, they were ordinary people who exercised extraordinary leadership when empowered by the God of surprises."[48] Kathy Khang adds an Asian American woman's perspective to the story of Esther: "She finds her voice, her identity, her power, and she speaks out against genocide, against the racist hate mongering, and she does it with strength and conviction and grace."[49]

Familial relationships are another central theme worth sharing from the pulpit. For example, Moses' mother resembles many ANA mothers, who are fiercely devoted to their children's ongoing welfare. Old Testament texts about passing on the faith from generation to generation, like Deuteronomy 6:1-9, are likewise relevant. The theme of honoring parents has strong biblical roots and also cultural connections. The book of Ruth has much to say about family

---

48   Tokunaga, *Invitation to Lead,* 106.

49   Kathy Khang, "Beauty Pageants & Bible Stories," *Kathy Khang* (blog), September 17, 2013, http://www.kathykhang.com/2013/09/17/beauty-pageants-bible-stories. Esther's voice and leadership is discussed further in Khang, *Raise Your Voice: Why We Stay Silent and How to Speak Up* (Downers Grove, IL: InterVarsity, 2018).

dynamics, especially on relating to one's mother-in-law. The parable of the prodigal son also has rich relevance for ANAs.[50] Daniel K. Eng explains how he has preached this parable:

> I spent purposeful time emphasizing how lost and out of place the younger son felt in the distant country, not fully accepted there or at home. I also spent time helping my audience understand the anger of the older son, who sees someone else getting a "handout" after he has worked so hard. These are both experiences that resonate with many Asian Americans.[51]

The theme of culture and identity is another fruitful avenue for exploration. Moses was a 1.5-generation person, born among the Hebrews but raised among Egyptians, who struggled with his cultural identity. Esther likewise was deeply assimilated but still of a particular ethnic group. While part of a minority within the larger Persian Empire, she was gifted and had an opportunity to make a difference.[52] The book of Acts, as it relates to culture and ethnicity, is another rich resource for ANA preaching. As the church developed in the first century, it faced a number of cultural issues similar to what ANA churches face today, such as the inclusion of gentiles in the church without their needing to become Jewish (Acts 10, 15). Acts 6:1–7 is a good case study of handling a church controversy with two cultural groups in the early church (Hebraic Jews versus Hellenistic Jews). This is comparable to the first-generation and second-generation Asians in a church. I preached in a Chinese church in Montreal to the English congregation with a number of first-generation parents and leaders present. In the early church, spiritually qualified and recognized

---

50 Daniel K. Eng, "Finally Belonging: The Reception of the Parable of the Prodigal Son Among Asian Americans," *The Journal of the Asian American Theological Forum* 6:2 (2019): 1–6.

51 Correspondence with Daniel K. Eng.

52 Tokunaga, *Invitation to Lead*, 106–22.

leaders were chosen to lead the group, not people who were older necessarily. It was important to challenge the congregation's precon-ceptions of who can serve the church as a leader and identify some of our inherent biases for and against certain groups of people.

Similar to the issue of cultural identity is the issue of esteem. What ANA hasn't been asked, "What are you?" As a Christian, who we are in Christ is paramount. The apostle Paul is a good example. He was a Hellenistic Jewish person and notes that he is what he is by the grace of God (1 Cor 15:10).

A final biblical theme that is commonly drawn out in ANA churches is that of social justice, especially among the younger gener-ation. They are seeing the bigger picture beyond their specific ethnic world. We are encouraged especially by the writings and presenta-tions of Soong-Chan Rah and Eugene Cho to take our mission field to the next level. Rah points out what we can learn from second-generation ANAs in "A Multicultural Worldview: Learning from the Second Generation."[53] He believes the second generation is leading the way for community involvement and crossing racial and cultural barriers. Cho tells an inspiring story of how he gave one year's salary for the sake of the poor and sublet his home and went couch surf-ing for ten weeks.[54] Ken Fong focuses on how to welcome LGTBQ people into a congregational setting, and his work is encapsulated in the Ken Fong Project.[55] We look forward to more movements in this direction that can have a local and global impact.

There are many more Scriptures and themes that could be drawn out and applied in an ANA context. If you are looking for a model for studying the Bible from an ANA perspective, Tom Lin has written an excellent resource, *Losing Face & Finding Grace: Bible Studies for Asian*

---

53   Soong-Chan Rah, *The Next Evangelicalism: Freeing the Church from Western Cultural Captivity* (Downers Grove, IL: InterVarsity, 2009), 180–99.

54   Eugene Cho, *Overrated: Are We More in Love with the Idea of Changing the World than Actually Changing the World?* (Colorado Springs, CO: David C. Cook, 2014). He is also the founder of the One Day's Wages movement.

55   The Ken Fong Project, http://kenfongproject-blog.tumblr.com.

Americans.[56] In it, he deals with a number of Scripture topics pertinent for preaching in ANA contexts. "A Party, for Me?" (Luke 15:11–24) and "Expectations" (Luke 15:25–32) are based on the parable of the prodigal son, with the first focusing on the younger son and the latter emphasizing the older son. "Idolizing the Family" (Matt 10:34–39 and Eph 6:1–3) explores the roles and relationships in the biblical family and the Asian American family. "Performance Orientation" (Luke 10:38–42) hits all of us who identify ourselves with the workaholic Martha rather than the contemplative Mary. "Toxic Shame" (John 8:2–11) explores the shame and loss of face common in Asian settings. The book includes stories and good questions that help readers examine Scripture from an ANA perspective. With a paucity of resources for Bible study written by ANAs, the general questions and leader's questions found in this book help provide ideas for studying Scripture with the ANA audience in mind.

In addition, special occasions such as weddings, funerals, baptisms, and child dedication services can be opportunities to highlight ANA, Asian, and Western cultures and experiences. Since multiple generations are in attendance, a wise word needs to be issued through preaching and pastoral care in these special moments.

PREACHING AND WORSHIP

While this book focuses on preaching, preaching is not done in isolation. The context for preaching is the church service, which usually begins and ends with worship. But is there such a thing as a distinct form of ANA worship? This question has been discussed in circles at places like InterVarsity and its Urbana conference, as well as at other conference settings. Russell Yee has argued that much of Asian American worship is Caucasian worship; he sees a need for more indigenous worship and has offered some suggestions and examples.[57]

---

56   Tom Lin, *Losing Face & Finding Grace: 12 Bible Studies for Asian Americans* (Downers Grove, IL: InterVarsity, 1996).

57   Russell Yee, "The Search for Asian American Worship."

The musical aspect of worship often expends as much time as the sermon or even more time. In my experience, the songs I've sung in ANA churches seem similar to other evangelical churches. A few ANAs have written songs that reflect their experience of God or their ANA perspective, and I would like to see more of this. For example, Kai Mark in Toronto has written several songs that have been sung in venues such as at Teens Conference.

In addition to lyrics, the instruments in worship may be used to reflect the ANA context. Many ANAs have musical training. I have known Chinese congregations to use Chinese instruments. Second-generation ANAs playing traditional Asian instruments would be an interesting addition to worship music.

Even if the style of music does not vary, other aspects of worship may reflect the ANA context. The ways songs are introduced or transitions are made can reflect the ANA experience. The content of the pastoral/intercessory prayers could reflect to a greater degree the struggles and tensions faced by ANAs. The images displayed on the screen or other artwork in the worship space could depict ANA culture. Of course, this does not need to be exclusive, but images that emerge from the ANA experience can be present.

Testimonies also can be used to enhance worship. A testimony of someone who has had an experience related to the central passage or theme can be added after the sermon. Hearing from an actual person rather than merely quoting someone in the sermon has a different and often more powerful dynamic.

I have briefly laid out a few ideas and possibilities, but more exploration needs to be done regarding ANA forms of worship. It may not be as distinct as African American or Latino church worship, but there should be some level of uniqueness in how ANAs as a group express themselves in worship. I look forward to seeing greater creativity in this area in the days to come.

CONCLUSION

In this chapter, we have looked at a wide variety of ANA preaching today, and I've articulated some common themes and characteristics. Just as ANA churches are composed of different ethnic groups, generations, and other human factors, ANA preaching is a mixed bag. In many ways, we could say that ANA preaching is amorphous. It seems like every church is just doing its own thing. What we need is a more focused approach to ANA preaching. How we get there is more intentional exegesis of the text, the congregation, and ourselves. I began this chapter by asking, what is the flavor or voice of ANA preaching today? Could you identify it if you heard an ANA preacher on the radio? My assumption is that in many second-, third-, fourth-, and fifth-generation ANA contexts, the answer would be no. The sermon would not explicitly or implicitly contextualize the message for ANA listeners.

We believe that ANA preaching requires an overhaul. Our ANA listeners are starving for contextualized sermons that unearth their questions, joys, and concerns with regard to exegesis, theology, illustrations, application, and more. What can we do in response? The future of ANA preaching awaits us in the final chapter.

QUESTIONS FOR REFLECTION
AND DISCUSSION

1. Recount your personal journey and how it affects your preaching.
2. How might you dig deeper into the biblical text with a view to preaching to ANAs?
3. What is your regular context for preaching?
4. How would you describe your preaching voice?
5. Who best exemplifies ANA preaching? What are some of the key characteristics?
6. What are ways to develop your preaching?

CHAPTER
FIVE

Matthew D. Kim and Daniel L. Wong

THE FUTURE OF ASIAN
NORTH AMERICAN PREACHING

T o this point, we have alerted you to ANAs' cultural experiences
and realities of living as ethnic minorities in North America,
raised hermeneutic and theological issues among ANA listeners, constructed a more balanced hermeneutic and theology for the ANA
context, and described the current landscape of ANA preachers and
their preaching. Where do we go from here? In this final chapter,
we will name some of our preferred distinctives of ANA preaching,
explore pertinent preaching topics that would benefit ANA listeners,
and conclude with some observations for the future of ANA preaching. We will attempt to answer the following big-ticket questions that
you've been patiently waiting for: What is our unique voice as ANA
preachers, and what contributions can we add to the homiletical
conversation? How does a specifically ANA homiletic benefit ANA
pastors and churches? And what will the future of ANA preaching
look like in our increasingly globalized world?

DISTINCTIVES OF ANA PREACHING

We believe that ANA preaching, like preaching in traditions associated with other minority groups, should be distinct in the areas of
hermeneutics, illustrations, applications, delivery, and in the choice
of topics to address. We will look at each of these in turn.

Hermeneutics

In chapter 2, Matthew stressed the importance of approaching biblical texts with an ANA hermeneutic. As noted there, everyone reads Scripture through the lens of particular experiences and cultures. Even the human authors of Scripture were not culture-free, but were immersed in and communicated out of a particular cultural background. Matthew encouraged ANA preachers, especially those trained in Western seminaries, to interpret Scripture using a hermeneutic that scans in a panoramic way the dual sides of the listeners—their Asian side and their American/Canadian side. Reading with an ANA hermeneutic means that we are sensitive to parallels and variances between ANA communities and the original audience as we read and study a passage.

Let's see how this might work in practice by taking the example of the prodigal son narrative in Luke 15. What similarities or incongruities exist in this passage between ancient Jewish culture and Asian/North American cultures? Matthew Williams, who teaches New Testament at Biola University, explains the Jewish context in this story: "In the first century … a Middle Eastern man never—never—ran. If he were to run, he would have to hitch up his tunic so he would not trip. If he did this, it would show his bare legs. In that culture, it was humiliating and shameful for a man to show his bare legs."[1]

As with the original audience, honor and shame is an important part of the ANA context, but perceptions of it change with the generations. While a white/North American dad might run toward his wayward child, the same scenario would not necessarily be true of stoic, East Asian dads. A traditional immigrant East Asian father, whether Chinese, Japanese, Korean, or other, probably would not run to his son, especially after the son had squandered his inheritance and brought tremendous shame upon the family name. However, in

---

1   Matthew Williams, "The Prodigal Son's Father Shouldn't Have Run," in *Biola Magazine,* Summer 2010, http://magazine.biola.edu/article/10-summer/the-prodigal-sons-father-shouldnt-have-run/.

most cases, a second- or third-generation ANA father would likely sprint as fast as he could to meet his wayward child, demonstrating more of a Western mindset. By articulating the differences in culture, we can guide our listeners who come from diverse familial backgrounds. Thus, an ANA hermeneutic would articulate the nuances among cultural and generational differences. An ANA hermeneutic takes the extra step to acknowledge not only the differences between ancient cultures and modern cultures, but also that there are variances across and within cultures. The ANA preacher takes into consideration the liminality and in-between-ness of their listeners. In the future, we look forward to Bible commentaries written by evangelical ANA scholars who can provide this additional perspective.

Illustrations

What kinds of illustrations would resonate most closely with ANA listeners? It's easy to preach to the generic American or Canadian— illustrating to the majority culture, whoever that majority might be in our congregation. That's what many of us have been trained to do in Bible college or seminary. Illustrations that speak to the ANA experience, however, will require a multipronged approach. Some ways that we can illustrate more broadly for our listeners who fall somewhere on the spectrum of being more North American or more Asian are by sharing personal stories, being careful to use both the right brain and the left brain, and celebrating ourselves and others.

First, both North American and Asian cultures are story cultures. You can't go wrong by telling a good, heartfelt, and inspiring story. One of the ways that ANA preachers can connect with ANA listeners is to offer self-disclosure in their illustrations while using spiritual discernment. It is natural to tell the stories of others and quote well-known authors and pastors, but it is less common for us to share our own testimonies and life experiences. There can be a sense of shame and vulnerability when confessing that we don't have all the answers or that we struggle at times with fear and doubt. Within reason, we can still share with our congregations how we are doing in life, faith, evangelism, and discipleship without celebrating and promoting sin and suspicion. Matthew still remembers the first time he shared a personal story in a sermon about his life. His church members connected immediately to his second-generation experience. While oversharing can be a danger, occasional personal stories enable us to find commonalities with our ANA hearers. Where else in North American society will they find such resonance with other ANAs?

Second, use both the right and left sides of the brain in your illustrations. Right-brain thinking commonly pertains to the arts, music, writing, and creativity, while left-brain thinking focuses on logic, math, reasoning, and computation. Increasingly, ANAs are not fitting the stereotypical mold of what it means to be a left-brained Asian who excels in math, science, medicine, engineering, business, accounting, and other more quantitative subjects. Illustrations about ANAs who receive perfect scores on the SAT, play the violin or piano, or work as a medical doctor, lawyer, engineer, or businessperson will only tell a smidgeon of the ANA cultural narrative. In fact, these types of illustrations tend to perpetuate the "model minority" stereotype: that ANAs work hard, are well-educated, work in professional careers, follow the rules, and represent the ideal minority group. Instead, we want to encourage a wide swath of illustration types for ANA hearers. Asians are also leading in entrepreneurship, acting, the arts, writing and literature, humanities and social sciences, music, fashion, and other more right-brained fields (think Vera Wang, Yo-Yo Ma, John Cho, and Ken Jeong). We invite you to use illustrations that connect with both brain types in your sermons. Find a way to incorporate and flex between right-brained and left-brained illustrations.

Third, use illustrations that celebrate both your culture and others. Oftentimes, our illustrations as ANA preachers vacillate between being self-promoting and self-loathing. A couple of Matthew's all-time favorite movies are *My Big Fat Greek Wedding* and its sequel. In many ways that are parallel with Asian ethnic groups, Greeks share a high sense of ethnic identity. Gus Portokalos, the Greek family head in the movie, champions to his children and grandchildren the importance of celebrating their Greek heritage. He says: "There are two kinds of people—Greeks, and everyone else who wish they was Greek." According to Gus, Greeks created everything of value and importance in the world in the areas of language, culture, art, and inventions. He even believes that the root of every word is Greek: "Kimono is come from the Greek word *himona,* is mean winter. So, what do you wear in the wintertime to stay warm? A robe. You see: robe, kimono. There you go!"

Sometimes we can sound like Gus, thinking that the world couldn't survive without our ethnic group. On the other hand, sometimes we fall into self-hatred and focus overly on the pejorative and destructive cultural patterns and sins of Chinese, Korean, and other Asian cultures. In our illustrations, we should avoid both of these extremes by committing to celebrating not just ourselves, but also others. Try to focus on the positives about ANA culture as well as regularly incorporating more illustrations that promote other ethnic groups and races.

Application

In one of Daniel's doctoral courses at Trinity Evangelical Divinity School, a fellow student articulated a new take on an old saying: "And all God's people said, 'So what?'" Everyone else in the class was startled at first, but then we realized that the question was on the hearts and minds of people in our congregations. Congregation members long for preachers to provide direction on how the Scripture applies to them. Otherwise, they find that sermons become more like Bible history lessons.

How might ANA preachers provide application in their sermons? Sermon application starts with the preacher. The preacher has the most conviction after wrestling with the biblical text for understanding and seeking application in his or her own life before preaching it.

This requires a commitment to begin preparation early in order to give the Holy Spirit time to convict you and apply the text to your own life. Of course, it is not always possible to have the preacher's experience apply directly to all types of people. A single person speaking on the topic of marriage, for example, can imagine what it's like but not have full knowledge. However, there can be indirect experience from speaking to others who are married and using that application in the sermon.

The preacher can also suggest avenues for application. These are concrete ways in which the text can be applied in the lives of the hearers. It is helpful to provide a variety of scenarios so that the examples are not restricted to one demographic and reflect the varied ANA experiences of your hearers. There can be something for students, something for a parent at home, and something for those working outside the home. It is important to note that individual avenues of application do not fulfill the requirements of the passage. Beyond an individual response is a collective or congregational response in song, prayer, or subsequent action. This is often absent from our preaching.

Finally, preachers can provide illustrations that help people envision how to apply the sermon in their lives. When people see themselves in an illustration, they can apply it in a similar situation. In one sermon, Daniel described how he bought an item from a store, gave the clerk ten dollars, and received change for twenty dollars. What should he have done? Should he have thought, "This is God's blessing of extra money" or, "It is too much trouble to alert the clerk?" In the end, he let the clerk know her mistake. The audience may have had the same or a similar experience where honesty is tested and hearing this story might help them decide what to do when faced with a circumstance like this in the future.

Application that is pertinent in ANA congregations is sometimes culturally specific and sometimes general. The important part is to use applications that connect with a range of your hearers so they can see how the sermon relates to them.

Delivery

While faithful and engaging sermon content should come first, how it is delivered enhances the overall effectiveness of the sermon. Delivery encompasses the verbal and visual aspects of the sermon, and both of these reflect the personality of the preacher. The typical ANA preacher's style tends to be more reserved and less expressive. This reservation in the pulpit occasionally has more to do with theological/denominational expectations than the preacher's ethnicity. In fact, there are ANA preachers who are known to be dynamic, engaging speakers: Francis Chan, Eugene Cho, James Choung, Dave Gibbons, Peter Hong, Dan Hyun, Ryan Kwon, Soong-Chan Rah, and others come to mind.[2] There is no right or wrong way to deliver a sermon in ANA contexts. Be who you are from the pulpit. However, Matthew often tells his students that you want the "best version of yourself" to stand in front of God's people to preach. Who are you in your most charming, charismatic, pastoral moments? What are you like when people enjoy your company? That's the person you want to step into the pulpit. Let's look at three aspects that ANA preachers could further develop to benefit their delivery.

First is the verbal component. Vocal variety is a key piece of the preaching puzzle. No one likes to hear a preacher droning on in a monotone voice. Variations in speed, emphases, and volume enhance the sermon. Well-timed pauses punctuate a sermon. The sermon needs progress and movement toward a clear destination. One of the ways we might enhance our vocal expression would be to wean ourselves from reading a sermon manuscript or being glued to an outline. Variance of vocal passion and facial expressions can be worked on by recording and listening to/watching our sermons. Practice ways to improve vocal variety and look for areas where your facial expressions don't seem to match the content of your message. Seek

---

2   See Ed Stetzer, "5 Asian-American Preachers Not Named Eugene Cho or Francis Chan ... and a Couple Who Are," *The Exchange with Ed Stetzer* (blog), *Christianity Today*, September 11, 2015, https://www.christianitytoday.com/edstetzer/2015/september/5-asian-american-pastors-not-named-cho-or-chan.html.

out assistance from other pastors in the area and even local preaching professors. In fact, Gordon-Conwell Theological Seminary offers a service for a fee called Sermon Rx, where preachers can send in a sermon manuscript/audio/video for positive and constructive evaluation from a preaching faculty member.

Second, the visual aspects of the sermon should be evaluated, including gestures and movement. Gesturing, mainly the use of the hands, assists in illustrating and drawing pictures in the minds of the listeners. It would be wonderful to see ANA preachers work on and hone their craft by using hand motions and even stepping away from the pulpit, when appropriate, to bring additional life to the sermon. Many ANA preachers are stoic, and some even read their sermons. Watch your sermon to see the ways you can improve your pulpit delivery through gestures and movement. Find ways to be more expressive and even incorporate some elements of theater/performance/acting to enliven the message. We are not asking you to be fake in the pulpit. And yet, there is room for growth and creativity among ANA preachers. For instance, Daniel took a course in seminary called "Effective Pulpit Delivery." It involved enacting a biblical story without notes. He learned about movement and staging, which boded well for future preaching. A number of preachers incorporate first-person narrative preaching in which you deliver the sermon as a Bible character.[3]

Third, personality provides the source of the verbal and visual components of the preacher's repertoire. Preachers have a natural cadence and rhythm. ANA pastors are not one size fits all by any means. Some ANA preachers have big personalities that fill the entire sanctuary while others are more docile. We all have a default delivery based on our personality, but we can work toward greater effectiveness by honing our verbal and visual elements. A common refrain

---

3   There are good resources for this type of preaching, like J. Kent Edwards, *Effective First-Person Biblical Preaching: The Steps from Text to Narrative Sermon* (Grand Rapids: Zondervan, 2005), and Haddon W. Robinson and Torrey W. Robinson, *It's All in How You Tell It: Preaching First-Person Expository Messages* (Grand Rapids: Baker, 2003).

that Matthew hears from preaching students is that they can't preach any differently because being introverted/shy/quiet is their innate personality. In other words, they're saying that they can't change. Indeed, God has created them in his image and with their specific personalities and skill sets, but we can't allow personality traits to limit us and become excuses for not developing our sermonic potential. Use your personality to its fullest, and in areas of weakness, push yourself out of your comfort zone so that, like Paul, we can say: "I become all things to all people so that by all possible means I might save some. I do all this for the sake of the gospel, that I may share in its blessings" (1 Cor 9:22b–23).

Preaching Topics

ANA preachers should also consider which preaching topics might best serve the ANA church. Many preachers plan out their sermon calendar based on books of the Bible or hot topics that they want to cover, and of course, these ways of planning sermons have their place and are necessary. We believe ANA preachers should not shy away from preaching any part of Scripture. Yet, as we decide what parts of Scripture to explore in our sermons, there are some topics that we would do well to return to again and again because of the outsize role they tend to play in ANA communities. Below we will look at five key topics: identity, shame and pain, God as Father, reconciliation and healing, and social justice.

First, identity is a prominent topic that needs to be preached about regularly in ANA congregations. Most congregation members, as well as the preacher, will struggle with this issue. It is important to stress that whatever the ethnic, racial, biracial, multiracial, or multicultural background, each individual is unique, made in the image of God. The starting place in speaking about identity is to accept ourselves and continue on in the Christian journey. Ultimately, finding our identity in Christ brings wholeness. We can then see purpose and relate to others out of a healthy self-esteem.

As discussed in chapter 4, biographical studies of Moses and Esther are particularly fertile ground for sermons that deal with identity. The apostle Paul's navigation of his own identity is also instructive. He was a Hellenistic Jew, familiar with the customs of both the Jews and the Greeks. He would become a Jew to the Jews and a Greek to the Greeks while retaining both cultures (1 Cor 9:20–22). Paul's protégé Timothy was biracial, having a Greek father and a Jewish mother (Acts 16:1). Other Scriptures that underscore our identity in Christ are 2 Corinthians 5:17 and Colossians 3:1–3.

In our global context, it is also important to see the bigger picture of identity. As Christians, the analogy of the body of Christ underscores that we are part of a larger believing community. Nevertheless, we are individual members of the whole. We can affirm the whole without obliterating the parts and the individual cultural dimensions. Both aspects are important as we work through our identity.

Second, every person on the planet lives with shame and pain to varying degrees.[4] In particular, Asians and ANAs harbor pain and shame consciously and subconsciously for most of their existence. Pain and shame are embedded from a young age in the DNA of ANAs. Children are shamed from early on simply for being Asian and having almond-shaped eyes; for wearing Korean brand-name shoes like Lottes instead of Nikes; for not solving a math problem quickly; for making a mistake and bringing shame on the family. The list goes on and on.

Pain is also a universal experience for ANAs. ANA children commonly experience the pain of growing up as latchkey kids whose parents are always working. Some kids can't remember the last time both of their parents ate a meal with them. ANA children are commonly bullied at school and in the world of social media (Facebook, Twitter, Snapchat, Instagram) for being Asian—often without parental awareness. An ANA child incurs the pain of racism, sexism, physical, verbal,

---

4   See Matthew D. Kim, *Preaching to People in Pain: Sharing Our Suffering in Sermons* (tentative title, Baker Academic, forthcoming).

and sexual abuse, and other harmful social interactions. ANA children want desperately to fit into a white-majority culture. Their pain runs deep on so many levels, and churches often neglect their struggles on Sunday morning.

Most, if not all, ANAs that we have spoken to and ministered to have difficulty letting go of their shame and pain. It sours their relationship with God. It taints how they view themselves. They feel unlovable and irredeemable. One of the ways that we can improve the spiritual quality of life of ANA listeners is to regularly preach on the grace and mercy of God. It may even be helpful to preach that it's okay to fail. The infamous suicide bridges at prestigious universities are commonly used as illustrations of pain and shame because ANAs and others can't cope with being somehow "less than" their peers. An ANA homiletic creates opportunities to speak biblical truth and wisdom into the shame and pain of our hearers.

Third, ANA preachers need to stress the fatherhood of God because the world lacks healthy father-child relationships as a whole. Sadly, it's not just a stereotype that many first-generation, 1.5-generation, and second-generation ANAs have strained or non-existent relationships with their earthly fathers and sometimes their mothers as well. We often feel like we must earn the love of our earthly fathers through worldly achievements. This relational strain is particularly acute between Asian dads and their sons. However, Ken Shigematsu provides encouragement when speaking of Sabbath observance: "My value doesn't come from what I produce but from the fact that I am loved by a perfect Father in heaven."[5] It's challenging to love our heavenly Father when we struggle to love our earthly fathers. The two relationships are often symmetrical.

Preaching on God as Father can be rather tricky. What's the difference between God the heavenly Father and our earthly father? How can we mend our relationships with both fathers? Gentleness

---

5　Ken Shigematsu, *Survival Guide for the Soul: How to Flourish Spiritually in a World that Pressures Us to Achieve* (Grand Rapids: Zondervan, 2018), 60.

and kindness are aspects of God the Father that we can highlight more intentionally in our preaching. When we think of a typical Asian dad, the most immediate character traits that come to mind are not gentleness and kindness. Many Asian dads love their children but do not know how to express their love. They can appear to be hot-tempered, easily angered, frustrated, harsh with their words, impatient, demanding, listening averse, stoic or emotionless, rarely articulating feelings, and more. To paint a portrait of our heavenly Father accurately will require finessing and teasing out the spectrum of who God is from holy, wrathful, and righteous to perfect, loving, and merciful. As we restore ANA listeners' relationships with God the Father, perhaps a switch will go off in their heads concerning their earthly fathers. As you preach, pray that the Spirit would mend broken family relationships in your congregation.

Fourth, the topics of reconciliation and healing need clear articulation in ANA congregations. Reconciliation with God is foremost (2 Cor 5:18; Col 1:20). The ANA preacher should communicate an ongoing reconciliation with God, including forgiveness and affirmation of our standing in Christ. The preacher may have a painful past that must be accepted and viewed from God's perspective. The preacher should encourage congregation members to be reconciled with God for salvation and ongoing relationship with the Creator.

Reconciliation with others is encouraged as well (Matt 5:23–24). The ANA preacher may harbor resentment against the senior pastor or senior leaders in the church. An atmosphere of mutual forgiveness must be cultivated. There is nothing more beautiful than when leaders and congregation members forgive each other and wash each other's feet.

Often there are extensive conflicts within congregations and among disparate family members. This commonly shows up in English-speaking ANA churches that share a building with a first-generation immigrant church. Due to language and cultural barriers, the English-speaking congregation and immigrant congregation battle miscommunication and misunderstandings. Nuclear families are also torn apart from festering parent-child conflict that cannot be resolved on its own. Racial reconciliation—between ANAs and whites, ANAs and blacks, ANAs and Latinos, and even among Koreans, Chinese, Hmong, Japanese, Filipinos, and other Asian groups—is a topic of conversation that would benefit from strategic time in the pulpit as ANA preachers guide their congregations in being instruments of grace and healing within and beyond ANA circles.

Finally, more ANA congregations are seeing their involvement in social justice issues as an imperative. Often these congregations are located in diverse communities. Once they open their eyes, they see social injustice around them. This follows the example of Jesus, who was moved with compassion when he saw the condition of people and encouraged prayerful and personal involvement to meet their needs (Matt 9:35–10:1).

Biblical responsibilities of social justice are highlighted in fulfilling the command to love God and neighbor (Mark 12:30–31). These neighbors include "the other" as dramatically illustrated in the story of the good Samaritan (Luke 10:25–37), which was an important role reversal. Social justice is also an outgrowth of the mandate of discipleship and part of following the example of Christ.

A preacher in an ANA congregation may address the topic of social justice by preaching through a book of the Minor Prophets or preaching a topical series. You might also explore passages of God's care for orphans and widows or preach on biblical characters like Ruth. You could point out Jesus' teaching or narrate Jesus' interaction with the marginalized like the Samaritan woman and the lepers that he cleansed.

Built into the preaching of social justice is practical application. Intimately connected to studying these topics is to live out Jesus' teaching, "Go and do likewise" (Luke 10:37). We need to embrace the challenge to care for those different than ourselves. Most ANA congregations are comfortable middle-class folks that have difficulty dealing with issues beyond their immediate congregation. Some ANA congregations do break out of their shells to help urban or inner-city ministries by volunteering to do things like serving food to the underprivileged. Other ANA congregations have formed ongoing relationships with Native American/Aboriginal/First Nations communities or have formed strategic missional partnerships in other locations. Serving in different settings helps to cultivate a heart of compassion and carry out the mandates of Scripture regarding justice.

Unquestionably, the preacher needs to take part in such initiatives, setting the example of personal involvement. Eugene Cho, the founder of One Day's Wages and former senior pastor of Quest Church in Seattle, underscores this: "I've been speaking, writing, blogging, and preaching about justice. It's easy to fall in love with the idea. But something gets lost in the actual practice and application."[6] Indeed, the preacher must practice what is preached!

These are some of the salient topics on which ANA preachers could spend a concerted effort to incorporate into the preaching calendar. They are poignant subjects that your congregants are working to make sense of, and addressing them in sermons will help ANAs to understand how God addresses them in Scripture.

DEVELOPMENT OF ANA PREACHING

ANA preaching is in a state of development. As such, ANA preachers are still finding and figuring out our homiletical voice. To this point, we have discussed some defining characteristics of ANA preachers and ANA preaching. The next step is to talk about other areas where ANA preaching can be a constructive influence and shape the discipleship of ANA Christians.

How can ANA preachers be a positive force for kingdom proclamation in the days ahead? Stated differently, how can ANA preachers

---

6   Eugene Cho, interviewed by Bethany Hoang, "Working for Justice Will Make You Uncomfortable," *Christianity Today,* September 23, 2014, https://www.christianitytoday.com/ct/2014/september/working-for-justice-will-make-you-uncomfortable.html. See Eugene Cho, *Overrated: Are We More in Love with the Idea of Changing the World Than Actually Changing the World?* (Colorado Springs, CO: David C. Cook), 2014.

encourage their congregations to be Christian leaders in an ever-changing culture? In this section, we would like to posit five areas for continuous development among ANA homileticians and preachers.

Preaching in a Prophetic Voice

While ANAs, at times, are the beneficiaries of positive perceptions like the model minority stereotype (discussed in chapter 1), ANAs must enter the difficult conversation of speaking out against racism and prejudice, particularly against African Americans, Hispanic Americans, and Native Americans/Aboriginal people.

We ANAs stand on the shoulders of civil rights activists who stood their ground before many of us set foot on North American soil. ANAs, while facing some real forms of discrimination and prejudice in North America, do not often have our very lives threatened like our African American brothers and sisters do for wrongs they have not committed. One of the leading ANA voices on this subject is Soong-Chan Rah. In his book *Prophetic Lament,* he challenges us to not merely lament, but actively challenge injustice: "A passive lament that fails to confront injustice fails to consider the power of prophetic advocacy in lament."[7] To love our neighbor means to speak up for the voiceless and those who need our defense. To love our neighbor means sacrificing our rights and freedom to care for the other person. To love our neighbor means not protecting our comfort, but seeking out opportunities to promote reconciliation, harmony, and peace.

Per capita, ANAs are the wealthiest ethnic minority group.[8] While more than 12 percent of Asian Americans do live at the poverty level,[9]

---

7 Soong-Chan Rah, *Prophetic Lament: A Call for Justice in Troubled Times* (Downers Grove, IL: InterVarsity, 2015), 208.

8 Jeff Guo, "The Asian American 'Advantage' That Is Actually an Illusion," *Washington Post,* December 29, 2016, https://www.washingtonpost.com/news/wonk/wp/2016/12/29/the-asian-american-advantage-that-is-actually-an-illusion/.

9 Victoria Tran, "Asian Americans Are Falling through the Cracks in Data Representation and Social Services," *Urban Institute* (blog), June 19, 2018, https://www.urban.org/urban-wire/asian-americans-are-falling-through-cracks-data-representation-and-social-services.

for those who possess material wealth, God has not blessed us simply to do as we please with his blessings. God calls ANAs to lead others to Christ and to serve others because of our prosperity and privilege. With our Asian face and North American citizenship, we can enter into countries where there is no gospel access for whites and others. We can use our God-given blessings to bring Christ's hope to the world. We can actively pursue social change by entering the volatile world of politics on local and national levels. We can speak up when other ethnic minorities are being mistreated, abused, profiled, and even threatened and killed. Preach with a prophetic voice and call out injustices and fight for the demonized and marginalized in our midst.

Preaching in a Multiethnic/Multicultural Context

Often ANA preachers receive opportunities to speak in settings that are multiethnic or multicultural. Multiethnic settings have a variety of ethnic groups but a similar culture while multicultural settings have various cultures represented. While English is often the language of communication, English is not the first language for many congregants who come from other countries. It is a privilege to speak to these congregations.

Elsewhere, Daniel has advocated for approaching the preaching task from the perspective of a missionary.[10] This involves developing sensitivity to all the cultures represented in the congregation. It means using a variety of illustrations and applications that resonate with pockets of the congregation.

ANA preachers already possess a heightened sense of ethnicity. We are a minority in the wider white culture. This makes it easier to connect with other minority groups. One caution is that we must be careful not to constantly deprecate Western culture. Otherwise, we may alienate those in the congregation from this background.

---

10   See Daniel L. Wong, "Preaching in a Multicultural World," *Preaching: The Professional Journal for Preachers,* 23:5 (March/April 2008): 12–16.

Take note that there may be congregants who are white but are first-generation immigrants from South Africa or Europe.

In our globalized world, it is not too far-fetched to imagine that multiethnic/multicultural preaching could eventually become the norm. In this kind of preaching, we recognize and affirm diversity but underscore what we hold in common. Through the internet and other means, the outside world impinges on even the most homogeneous congregation. Sometimes it is the extent of diversity that is the difference. These are the contexts in which we are carrying out our preaching.

Reenvisioning ANA Worship

ANA preaching is carried out mainly within the framework of an ANA worship service. Just like with ANA preaching, there is a question about the distinctiveness of ANA worship. Much of this worship contains Western contemporary worship songs and expressions but with Asian faces.

Just as we look forward to ANA preachers finding their distinct voice, we anticipate a time when ANA worship will be distinct as well. This will go beyond the mere preponderance of Asian faces leading worship. We would like to see different or enhanced styles and expressions. We look forward to hearing more songs that express the ANA experience. There should also be other outlets for worship such as drama, dance, art, poetry, rap, and the spoken word.

Russell Yee is one of the leading thinkers today on ANA worship.[11] Just as missionaries find ways to contextualize the Bible, the gospel, and the sacraments for local people, Yee encourages ANA pastors to use creativity to speak to what is often called the "heart language" of ANA people through worship. This doesn't mean that we slip in traces of Asian spirituality like being mystical or practicing transcendental meditation or bringing other religious practices

---

11 Russell Yee, *Worship on the Way: Exploring Asian North American Christian Experience* (Valley Forge, PA: Judson, 2012).

into the ANA worship service. Rather, he encourages ANA pastors to guide worshipers toward a more contextualized worship style. For example, ANA listeners might pray not with their eyes closed and head bowed (the Western mode of prayer), but with a posture that is respectful for Asian contexts such as kneeling or "bowing to the ground" or even with one's "face to the floor."[12]

ANA worship should be contextualized throughout the entire service, including the songs we sing, the prayers that are prayed, how Scripture is read, how the offering is collected, how sacraments are performed, and how preaching is done.

Building a Racial and Ethnic Bridge

The beauty of diversity is that no single culture holds a monopoly on who God is. Just as we can never enter into our children's bodies and put our brains inside of their heads, the same limitations exist for ANAs and people from other ethnic/racial groups. We don't live the Christian life in a bubble, even in predominantly ANA congregations. Most likely, your ANA congregation is not completely homogeneous; the diversity spans various racial and ethnic groups. To preach in ANA congregations in the future will mean building a racial and ethnic bridge with our congregants.

One of the longest suspension bridges in the world resides in Japan. Called the Akashi-Kaikyo Bridge, it is nearly 13,000 feet in length and conjoins an island to the mainland. The bridge took about forty years to be designed and constructed.[13] Creating and building physical bridges does not happen overnight. It takes much thought and perpetual diligence. In a similar way, building bridges across different races, ethnicities, and cultures is a daunting process. In some ways, it's easier to build a physical bridge than a relational one. Yet God calls ANA pastors and preachers to develop friendships across

---

12   Yee, *Worship on the Way,* 5–6.

13   See Soo Kim, "The World's Longest Bridges—Where Would Boris Bridge Rank?," *Telegraph,* January 19, 2018, https://www.telegraph.co.uk/travel/lists/worlds-longest-bridges/.

racial/ethnic lines. In our role as pastors, preachers, and teachers, and depending on our geographic location, we are constantly meeting people from different cultures. Building a bridge with others takes time, resources, intentionality, and most importantly sacrifice. Matthew has written elsewhere about the ways that preachers can invest energy to learn more about diverse listeners.[14] This includes not just reading about other cultures, but actually spending time in other cultures, learning words and phrases in other languages, eating other cuisines, listening to music from other cultures, going to cultural celebrations and ceremonies, and more.

Some ANAs may want to preserve ethnic or racial identity in the church by maintaining homogeneity or at least their "pan-Asian-ness." After all, it may be the only place where we feel empowered and comfortable living in a white-majority society. At the same time, perhaps God created us as bicultural and sometimes multicultural people so that we can stand in the gap between ethnic minorities and a predominantly white North America. While some ANA churches are called to minister primarily to the ANA community, every Christian is called to build human bridges with people that we meet. How can ANA preachers minister and preach in such a way that we build bridges with others? Put differently, what are the possible selves of ANA Christians?

Envisioning the Possible Selves of ANAs

During his doctoral studies, Matthew came across a social psychology construct called the possible selves theory. Developed in 1986 by University of Michigan scholars Hazel Markus and Paula Nurius, the possible selves theory explored people's fears, hopes, and expectations.[15] Matthew later added a spiritual component to the possible selves theory specifically for second-generation Korean Americans.[16]

---

14   See, for example, Kim, *Preaching with Cultural Intelligence.*

15   Hazel Markus and Paula Nurius, "Possible Selves," *American Psychologist,* 41 (1986): 954–69.

16   See Kim, *Preaching to Second Generation Korean Americans,* 129–60.

While the possible selves theory has its own limitations, something we can consider for the future of ANA preaching is the possible selves of our ANA church members.

What do our listeners fear, hope for, and expect for themselves now and in the future? Another way of naming possible selves could be exploring visions, dreams, or aspirations. Whether or not you have been the primary voice that speaks into their lives, every single listener in your church has visions, dreams, and aspirations. Sometimes they are articulated and sometimes they are not. One vision for the future of ANA homiletics regards dreaming and casting a vision.

Every single week you can help your listeners move from selfish and materialistic dreams to selfless and heaven-focused visions for their lives. Many of our ANA listeners have bought into the narrative of the American or Canadian dream. When Jesus said in John 10:10, "I have come that they may have life, and have it to the full," many ANAs have literally focused on having an earthly, materially full life. We can, however, biblically inspire and inform our listeners to create new possible selves that are biblical, God-centered, kingdom-building, and discipleship-oriented. What would it look like for our ANA church members to be fulfilling the Great Commission and using their time, talents, and treasures for kingdom expansion?

These visions and dreams don't have to be grandiose or highfalutin. Equip them to live out the gospel in the mundane tasks of life. As Tish Harrison Warren invites us to consider in her book *Liturgy of the Ordinary*, "The crucible of our formation is in the anonymous monotony of our daily routines."[17] Help your listeners each week by facilitating the imagining of their possible selves. Encourage them to pursue holiness, righteousness, mercy, justice, the fruit of the Spirit, the humility found in the Beatitudes, purity, gospel ministry, evangelism, discipleship, and so much more. Help them forgive

---

17   Tish Harrison Warren, *Liturgy of the Ordinary: Sacred Practices in Everyday Life* (Downers Grove, IL: InterVarsity, 2016), 34.

others for the pain they have experienced as ANAs who have been marginalized and discriminated against on various levels. Help them build bridges with others from different ethnicities and races. ANAs have been blessed by God to be a blessing on this earth. Impress that truth on your listeners.

CONCLUSION: CELEBRATE YOUR ANA-NESS

As we have cast a vision for the future of ANA preaching, we hope we have reinforced your belief that ANA cultures have a lot to bring to the table. There are clear reasons why God created the people group known as Asians. We want to take time to celebrate our ANA cultures. Paul Tokunaga shares: "Asian [North] Americans have gifts to bring to the party. Our gifts are important as well as unique. We have some gifts that no one else can bring. ... There are some wonderful aspects of being Asian [North] American that give us special contributions to make to the kingdom."[18]

God has a special plan for ANA Christians. He wants to use our bicultural and multicultural experiences to help build his kingdom. Through the proclamation of God's word, we can help ANA Christians find their voice in the world. We can show them how to grow in their Christlikeness as ANA disciples and how they can contribute in expanding God's mission around the globe.

There is so much more to discover and uncover on the topic of ANA preaching; its depths are still to be plumbed. We are praying that you will join us in finding our voice as ANA preachers. Each time you press into what it means to be Asian and Canadian/American, you are holistically engaging your listeners' myriad worlds. Preaching cannot remain in the world of generalities. We cannot assume that generic sermons reach our listeners. As we preach with greater cultural awareness and sensitivity for ANA cultures, they will come to

---

18   Paul Tokunaga, "Gifts Asian Americans Bring," in *Following Jesus without Dishonoring Your Parents,* by Jeanette Yep, Peter Cha, Susan Cho, Van Riesen, Greg Jao, and Paul Tokunaga (Downers Grove, IL: InterVarsity, 1998), 161–62.

a richer understanding of who God has created them to be as ANA people. They will begin to shepherd, guide, and disciple fellow ANAs and others in the Christian life. It's our collective prayer that God will use present and future generations of ANA preachers and ANA Christians to expand his kingdom. To God be the glory.

QUESTIONS FOR REFLECTION AND DISCUSSION

1. Which ANA preaching distinctives would you like to explore in greater depth (e.g., hermeneutics, illustrations, application, or delivery)?

2. Which preaching topics (e.g., identity, shame and pain, God as father, reconciliation and healing, and social justice) have you preached on and which one(s) would you like to develop in the near future that would benefit your congregation? How will you accomplish this?

3. Which ANA preaching area (e.g., preaching in a prophetic voice, multiethnic/multicultural preaching, worship, building a racial and ethnic bridge, or the possible selves of ANAs) would you develop in the near future? How do you intend to do this?

4. How do you see ANA preaching developing in the future?

5. What might be your role in shaping the future of ANA preaching?

6. Reflecting on your preaching voice, how has it developed over time and which areas would you like to develop in the future?

7. Give thanks for the background, experiences, and gifts God has given you. How do you envision God using you in the future?

APPENDIX ONE

WORKSHEET FOR
ANA PREACHING

Sermon Text: _____

Main Idea: _____

HERMENEUTICS

What questions, assumptions, and concerns does this text raise for my ANA listeners?

Questions:

Assumptions:

Concerns:

THEOLOGY

1. What does this text say about God that is relevant from an Asian perspective?

2. What does this text say about God that is relevant from a North American perspective?

APPLICATION

1. In light of this text, what do my listeners need to know?

2. What do my listeners need to be?

3. What do my listeners need to do?

4. How do my listeners need to grow?

5. Which applications in this passage focus on the individual, and what can apply to the entire church?

6. What applications are really misapplications in this text?

ILLUSTRATIONS

1. Which types of illustrations work best for this sermon that include Asian and North American cultures?

2. Write down three to five illustration possibilities. How do these illustrations connect with Asian and/or North American experiences?

PREACHING TOPICS

1. How might this text speak to issues of identity?

2. How might this text address shame and pain?

3. What prophetic word does this text call for?

4. How might this text help us build a bridge across races and ethnicities?

5. List two to three possible selves that you can encourage listeners to envision or dream for themselves in this sermon.

APPENDIX TWO

SAMPLE SERMONS

B y sharing these sermons preached in ANA congregations, we offer a sample of contextualized ANA preaching that exegetes, illustrates, and applies Scripture for ANA listeners. While no sermon is ever perfect, we hope that these will serve as a guide for how we can speak to both Asian and North American cultures in our preaching.

Matthew D. Kim

MIND RENEWAL
ROMANS 12:1–3

A sermon delivered to an ANA congregation in Denver, Colorado.[1]

Main Idea: A life of transformation starts with a renewed mind.

INTRODUCTION

Something that has become very popular in today's media-crazed society is a fascination with virtual online communities. In a recent article, Rachel Konrad writes about Cyworld Inc., a Korean-based website that is making its way to the US. Henry Chon, the CEO of Cyworld, says: "Once Americans see the value of Cyworld, they'll make sure their friends and family use it. ... We're here to build a meaningful, good community."

"Cyworld is a parallel universe unto itself," Konrad writes. "It combines aspects of 'simulated reality' computer games ... with massively multiplayer online games that have thousands of players facing off simultaneously in what's known as a 'persistent world.' But Cyworld isn't a game; the goal isn't to slay dragons or amass points but to socialize with 'cybuddies.'" This website "emphasizes relationships

---

1 This sermon was originally published on PreachingToday.com. Adapted and used by permission. See https://www.preachingtoday.com/sermons/sermons/2010/july/renewalofthemind.html.

between relatives, neighborhood friends, and co-workers—people who have already met in real life but yearn to also hang out online."

Cyworld is a sign of the times. More and more, our world has become impersonal. It's easier to hang out with friends in an online virtual world than to have face-to-face interaction at a coffee shop. We have become less interactive with our family members and friends. We'd rather chat with someone online than make a heart-warming visit to someone's home.

I once heard a story about a family where each person had a computer in his or her own bedroom, and the kids would chat online with each other and their parents instead of sitting in a room talking face to face. I wonder if the church has followed the ways of this world and become more virtual than real. How can we reclaim community in the church today?

In Romans 12:1-3, the apostle Paul offers some practical steps for us to truly grow as a community of brothers and sisters in Christ. Specifically, we will spend our time focusing on areas concerning this passage where we struggle as Asian Americans and how we can respond to Paul's invitation to live a life of transformation into the image of Jesus.

1. WE ARE ONE BODY AND ONE FAMILY

Paul loved the Romans deeply. He longed to visit them in person as we read in Romans 1:11. Throughout this letter, Paul refers to the Romans as his brothers, members of one body which is his spiritual family. Now, in Romans 12:1-3, the affection that Paul has for the Romans urges him to remind his spiritual family members to live differently from the rest of the world. Since they are "family," Paul feels compelled to call out their worldly attitudes especially toward worship and in their patterns of thinking.

We may look around the sanctuary and say, "That person is not like me. We don't look alike. We don't have the same interests." But

God says we are one body through our common faith in Jesus Christ. No family is perfect, but we do belong to each other.

Most people love their families. Let's start with parents. We love our parents, but as we all know, our parents can drive us crazy. They know exactly what to do and say that will "push our buttons." There are times that we have cursed at our parents, we've said hurtful things to them, and we've embarrassed them in public. Yet, at the end of the day, the common trait that binds us together is that we share the same blood. For this very reason, we love them no matter how much they make us mad. Despite how much they hurt us, we love them.

The same holds true for those of us who have brothers and sisters. Growing up, I fought a lot with my two younger brothers. Things got messy in a household of three boys. We would punch each other. We put holes in the walls with our fists because we were so mad at each other. We were, at times, very cruel with our choice of words. No family is perfect, and there is no way that we can always get along. But if anyone ever tried to hurt either of my brothers, there is nothing that I wouldn't do to save them.[2] I would give my life for them. Why? Because they are my brothers! We share the same blood.

I want us to take a look around the room for a minute. What I have just shared with you about my family is the same for us here in this room. We are family. No matter how much we may think the person next to us has nothing to do with us, we are family because we share the same blood, the blood of Christ.

Today, I would like for us to rethink what it means to be a church. Rather than thinking that we are nonrelated people from all walks of life, I'd like us to think of ourselves as one big family—one household of God. Despite the fact that we may dislike or be displeased with another person sitting here in the sanctuary, we share the same blood, making us family. We are to love our family members, for each person is significant—just like our immediate family members.

---

2   Since the time when this sermon was given, Matthew's brother, Timothy David Kim (1979–2015), was murdered in Manila, Philippines.

A. Members of God's family offer their bodies as living sacrifices.

Paul says: "Therefore, I urge you, brothers, in view of God's mercy, to offer your bodies as living sacrifices, holy and pleasing to God—this is your spiritual act of worship." For those of us who have read the Old Testament, we know that in order to be cleansed from sin, people needed to sacrifice animals without defect. The Jews gave a sin offering to God and sacrificed animals on behalf of their sin. The sin would be transferred to that animal and would be offered up in lieu of the people.

In this passage, we come to truly understand the mercy of God. Not only did animals need to be sacrificed for their blood, but also we were the ones who were supposed to lay down on the altar of sacrifice for our own sins. Our sins deserved death (Rom 6:23). But, rather than continuing animal sacrifices and having us pay the penalty of death, Jesus Christ, the sinless one, took on our sin and sacrificed his very life for us. When we understand this profound truth, our gratitude for God's mercy would overflow into us willingly offering every part of our lives as a "living sacrifice" for God. The act of worship is not just giving an hour on Sunday. It's laying down our entire lives on the altar as being completely available to serve God in whatever he calls us to be and to do.

In order to learn and grow as a community, it is time that we earnestly contribute to the work of the body of Christ. Being "living sacrifices" means that we get out of the comfortable mode of "feed me" and "serve me," to "I'll feed others and serve others." Through our service to God, we worship him.

I want to make it clear that God does not need us to serve him, but he knows that it is good for our hearts. It is for our benefit that we serve God. God can do whatever he pleases, but through offering our lives in service to God, we please him!

In any community, the group functions most effectively when every person contributes. So it is with the church. The church can function at its best when people serve. Church experts say that 80 percent of the work in churches is done by 20 percent of the members. According to George Gallup, only 10 percent of all people in church are active in a ministry. An additional 50 percent of the people have no interest in serving. Forty percent said that they'd like to be involved but have never been asked or told how to serve.

How does Paul say we can offer our bodies as living sacrifices? How can each of us get involved? Verses 6–8 state how we can help each other learn to grow in community.

B. Like every family, Paul says we have different gifts.

In verse 6, Paul specifically mentions seven spiritual gifts: (1) prophecy, (2) service, (3) teaching, (4) encouragement, (5) giving, (6) leadership, and (7) mercy. Let me concisely define each of these gifts, using selected material from James R. Edwards's commentary on Romans.

Prophecy is "offering guidance from the Spirit or God's Word in particular circumstances."

Service literally means "to wait on tables." Notice that service comes before teaching, which is "instruction in the whole counsel of God."

Encouragement is not only cheering someone up, but also being a "helpful companion." A person gifted in encouragement is someone who serves alongside of another person.

"Giving generously" is the spiritual gift of freely sharing God-given resources of time and money.

Leadership in the church is the ability to inspire others to believe in and act on the same Christ-honoring goals and visions.

Finally, mercy is the ability to have great compassion for others in difficult circumstances.

God equips each person with at least one spiritual gift. In order to become a healthy learning and growing community, we need to become a family of God and learn about our gifts and use them as living sacrifices offered to God.

2. UNLEARN NEGATIVE AND
HARMFUL VIEWS OF THIS WORLD

Paul also says in verse 2: "Do not conform any longer to the pattern of this world, but be transformed by the renewing of your mind." He is inviting us to a life where we are no longer controlled by the systems of the world and how the world thinks and operates.

For many of us, it means that we unlearn the negative and harmful patterns of Korean/Asian culture. Although there are various positive influences of Korean/Asian culture—such as respect, honoring elders, and values of education—there are an equal number of negative values and philosophies that affect Asian American Christians in different ways, hampering our ability to grow in community. In many ways, we are expected in Asian cultures to conform to the will of the larger body, whether that's our parents, immediate family, extended family, or wider Korean or Chinese cultures. But it's only when we conform to the will of God and not to the pattern of Asian or American societies that we will be able to "test and approve what God's will is—his good, pleasing, and perfect will" (Rom 12:2).

In their book, *Growing Healthy Asian American Churches,* the authors discuss various stumbling blocks for Asian American churches in becoming healthy communities. Helen Lee writes specifically about Confucian-based ideologies, concerning hierarchy and patriarchy in the forms of ageism and gender bias. There is a tendency, even among Americanized Asians, to look down on those who are younger and to say women cannot do certain things because of their gender.

Lee also discusses Asian Americans' propensity toward false humility—the tendency to avoid leadership positions because of their "I am not worthy" mentality. Nancy Sugikawa, a pastor at Lighthouse Christian Church in Washington says, "When I was at a primarily Caucasian church recruiting potential small group leaders, I found that people volunteered easily—even those who were new Christians or had never even been in a small group before. They were willing to try leading, even if it meant risking failure or rejection. In Asian churches, people rarely volunteer for leadership positions. You have to personally approach and encourage them. Non-Asians seem to handle rejection better. If Asians are not accepted into leadership after volunteering, they often feel a sense of shame or inadequacy, which might prevent them from ever volunteering again."

Citing Moses as an example, the authors of *Growing Healthy Asian American Churches* recognize two major things that Asian Americans need to learn: (1) It is very clear that "leaders do not always excel in all areas," and (2) whatever deficiencies leaders may have, "every leader has shortcomings that God can more than compensate."

There is a third and final obstacle for Asian American churches. Paul Tokunaga, the Asian American Ministry Coordinator for InterVarsity Christian Fellowship, says, "More than anything, those of us from shame-based cultures need to know and experience God's unconditional, unearnable love."

Pastor Emeritus Ken Fong of Evergreen Baptist Church of Los Angeles describes two types of shame: healthy shame and toxic shame. He writes: "Healthy shame is an intermittent, proper awareness of being a limited, flawed human being. It leads to the acknowledgement of your need for help from a higher power. It is the source of creativity. It is the core of true spirituality. ... Toxic shame, on the other hand, is the dark feeling that you are flawed as a human being. In spite of your efforts to change, deep inside, it feels hopeless because you do not believe that genuine change is truly possible. After all, you did not just make a mistake; you *are* the mistake."

How many of us struggle with toxic shame? Are we ashamed of who we are? Are we ashamed of what we have become? Are we ashamed of our backgrounds? Can we be a community of grace that embraces each person simply because they are loved by God?

In learning to grow as a community of God, it is crucial that we unlearn the things of the world that prevent us from becoming the person God has called us to be.

3. WE ARE TO BE TRANSFORMED
BY THE RENEWING OF OUR MINDS

Romans 12:3 says: "For by the grace given me I say to every one of you: Do not think of yourself more highly than you ought, but rather think of yourself with sober judgment, in accordance with the measure of faith God has given you." The world's pattern is to champion a very high view of self. We are expected to boast in our accomplishments. We were the ones who worked hard for what we enjoy, such as our educations, jobs, prestige, or status. But Paul instructs the Romans and us to be sober-minded as God provides the faith toward greater humility. Part of renewing our minds involves sober judgment so that we can work together as the body of Christ. How can I work with someone or serve them when I think I'm better than them?

Although many of us may struggle with the "I'm not worthy" syndrome, there are an equal number of us who are members of the "I'm too good for this church" mentality. How many of us, at the core of our being, feel that we are too good to serve or too good for others? Paul wants us to reconsider how good we really are and to think of ourselves in sober judgment.

One of the primary barriers to healthy growth as a church community is pride. Everything has to be our way because we're the best. We know how things should operate. We know who should be in leadership and who shouldn't. We know who should serve in what capacity. These attitudes of superiority can either reflect Asian ethnocentrism or American pride. We know best.

If we desire to become a learning and growing church community, we must let go of our pride. We must instead choose to love others and be humble before others. This means we don't always speak our minds at gatherings, but we listen to others' voices and opinions. It means we show our appreciation for people who are serving in different roles for the sake of the body of Christ. It means encouraging others and helping them grow.

One of the primary ways we will grow as a church is to see ourselves as a family where each member loves and serves each other. This means we put others first in our minds and in our actions. This means we believe we are no better or worse than the person sitting next to us. This means we treat visitors well by welcoming them. This means that we see others through the eyes of Jesus.

CONCLUSION

Interestingly, the reason why Alcoholics Anonymous has been so successful is because each person in the group recognizes he or she is an alcoholic and needs the help of both God and others to stay sober. In the church, the same principle holds true. If we are to grow as a community, we must renew our minds in learning to depend on God, in becoming vulnerable with each other, in unlearning our destructive Korean/Asian values, overcome shame, and in remembering we need each other and are dependent on each other for growth. A life of transformation starts with a renewed mind.

It is my prayer that we offer our bodies as living sacrifices, where we seek to be transformed and renewed in our minds, where people encourage others to serve and exhibit humility. Remember this week that a life of transformation starts with a renewed mind.

Daniel L. Wong

WHO AM I? WHAT AM I?
2 CORINTHIANS 4:7–18

*A sermon delivered to an ANA congregation in the
Toronto metropolitan area.*

**Main Idea: God uses ordinary people like us to carry out
the ministry of the gospel.**

INTRODUCTION

Who am I? Have you asked yourself this? Our identity is often defined by our achievements, degrees, position, or by our children. Most of us are Asian, living in the Greater Toronto Area, and born in Canada. I'm sure you have been assumed to belong to another Asian group or even to be a non-Asian. This is particularly true if your last name is "Lee," which can be a Chinese, Korean, white, or black last name.

You may have also asked yourself: What am I? Others have tried to figure you out. They may start speaking to you in Chinese or Korean. Some have greeted me in Korean in Korean churches and in Galleria Supermarket.[1] I politely nod in response. We English-speaking Asians have to navigate the multicultural terrain in our area and in Canada.

---

1   Galleria Supermarket is a popular Korean food store chain in the Toronto metropolitan area.

I wonder if the apostle Paul had such an experience. He was Jewish but not raised in a primary cultural area of the Jews. He is Paul of Tarsus; not Paul of Jerusalem. He was Joe from Toronto, not Joe from Seoul or Beijing. His main language was Greek and not Aramaic, which the Hebrews spoke. Was he criticized for not always speaking Aramaic?

The apostle Paul was criticized by others in a number of ways. Other teachers said he didn't measure up. How could he be an apostle, a messenger from God? What happens when you don't fit the stereotype? The apostle Paul faced criticism. Into the church of Corinth came false teachers who questioned the character and the authority of Paul. They questioned his word as he had seemingly changed travel plans to visit the church. They questioned whether he had pocketed the offering destined for the poor Christians in Jerusalem. They questioned if he was really God's messenger, an apostle.

The apostle Paul responds in what we know as 2 Corinthians regarding these charges. He is not aiming to defend himself, but to defend the gospel and the Lord Jesus Christ whom he proclaimed. He did not boast in himself; he was a "sent one," an apostle. The ones he writes to are special too. They are called "holy people" in 2 Corinthians 1:1, or "saints."[2] This is one of the most personal of Paul's letters. As we read through the letter, we get a sense of his heartbeat. It is the heart of someone who serves. He is someone we should follow as he follows Christ (1 Cor 11:1).

So in facing criticism, Paul defends himself and his calling. In doing this, he is not defensive or offensive, but sets forth himself and his message.

---

2   English Standard Version and most other Bible versions.

1. WE ARE ORDINARY CONTAINERS
(2 Cor 4:7–11, 16; cf. 2 Cor 11:23–28)

Who communicated the gospel message to the Corinthians? What was their message? "We have this treasure in jars of clay" (2 Cor 4:7). Today's preachers are often pictured in expensive clothing and having lavish lifestyles. Paul describes the messenger in humble terms: "jars of clay." Earthen vessels or jars of clay were storage jars, simple and fragile, just everyday ware. A lamp was made of clay to hold oil and a wick.[3] These are unlike the pristine, kiln-fired porcelain vessels that you find in the Royal Ontario Museum. Clay jars could be used to hold garbage. They also could be used to hold valuables. The Dead Sea Scrolls were found in clay jars.

Paul is saying that pastors and all of us are ordinary containers. Some people think they are indispensable, superstars, up on pedestals, yet we are all ordinary clay pots. The ground is level at the foot of the cross.

Here is a flower pot. It is made of clay. It is quite ordinary. It was purchased at a local store. Here is a rice bowl. It is found in homes or restaurants for everyday usage. This one is made of plastic. It is quite common and ordinary.

Paul underscores the frailty of the messenger with a series of paradoxes. From verses 7–12: "But we have this treasure in jars of clay to show that this all-surpassing power is from God and not from us. We are hard pressed on every side, but not crushed; perplexed, but not in despair; persecuted, but not abandoned; struck down, but not destroyed. We always carry around in our body the death of Jesus, so that the life of Jesus may also be revealed in our body. For we who are alive are always being given over to death for Jesus' sake, so that his life may also be revealed in our mortal body. So then, death is at

---

3   Homer A. Kent, *A Heart Opened Wide: Studies in Second Corinthians* (Grand Rapids: Baker, 1982), 72.

work in us, but life is at work in you." William Barclay puts it this way: "We are knocked down but not knocked out."[4]

Paul goes on to describe what else he faced as an apostle, as one sent with a message, later in 2 Corinthians 11:23–28: imprisoned for his faith, flogged, exposed to death, beaten, stoned, shipwrecked, danger from bandits and from his own countrymen, false believers, sleepless nights, hunger, thirst, frigid cold, nakedness, and besides everything else, he faced daily the pressure of his concern for all the churches. Many of us can identify with the emotional toll experienced in caring for others as we work with them for the sake of the gospel. There is effort, misunderstanding, and emotional toil to pray and weep over others to follow Christ.

Our passage encourages that we should not lose heart though we are "outwardly wasting away" (2 Cor 4:16). As human frail servants of God, we feel our mortality. This is an experience we all face. In one *Kim's Convenience* episode called "Appa's Lump,"[5] the father ("Appa" in Korean) finds a lump on his back. This points to one of the serious themes of the series, exploring life and mortality. We are getting older, and we can't do things like we used to. We can't lift the same weights as before. When a funeral procession passes by, we slow down and reflect on life.

We are ordinary containers. We are frail. But the hope is that inwardly we are being renewed day by day (2 Cor 4:16).

2. WE HOLD A POWERFUL MESSAGE
(2 Cor 4:12–15; cf. Rom 1:16; 1 Cor 15:1–4)

Within this frail container, we hold a powerful message. It is the contents of the container that are important. Here is a flower pot. It can contain a well-bred orchid. The rice bowl can hold delicacies

---

4   "William Barclay's *Daily Study Bible: 2 Corinthians 4*," StudyLight.org, https://www.studylight.org/commentaries/dsb/2-corinthians-4.html.

5   "Appa's Lump" is season 1, episode 12, of the Canadian television comedy *Kim's Convenience* (aired December 27, 2016).

like abalone. So we have this "treasure" in an ordinary container. *The Message* expresses it this way: "We carry this precious Message around in the unadorned clay pots of our ordinary lives" (2 Cor 4:7). That message is described as "the light of the knowledge of the glory of God in the face of Christ" (2 Cor 4:6). It is the gospel, the good news or message of the death, burial, and resurrection of Christ. The gospel is the power of God to save for those who believe (Rom 1:16). It is described in 1 Corinthians 15:1–4. The focus is on the gospel.

In 2 Corinthians 4:12–15, Paul points to the power of the spoken word. He quotes Psalm 116:10 to support speaking or testifying based on our beliefs. We also testify of a transformed life, particularly our inward lives are being renewed or changed (2 Cor 4:16). Have you had the thrill of sharing your testimony of how you came to Christ?

This gospel power, it's not of ourselves, but it is from God. I think of the experience when we share Christ with others, when we share our testimony. We tell people we go to church, and they ask, "Why do you go to church?" We respond, "Something happened in my life and is happening in my life." And that's the power of the gospel, the resurrected Christ, which is active in each of our lives. In the early part of this chapter, it speaks about the gospel when it is hidden or veiled; it's veiled to those who are perishing; the God of this age has blinded the mind of the unbeliever so that they cannot see the light of the gospel and the glory of God. I know we're all struggling to share Christ with others. We know we've experienced our salvation, but it's difficult to articulate that to a coworker, classmate, a friend, a neighbor, or to a family member.

As God works in us, you can't keep silent. It's as if you found a BOGO (buy one, get one) at the local bubble tea shop. You directly message friends and you post it on social media. You want others to experience it as well. It's the same thing with the gospel when we have experienced life-changing salvation in Christ. We can share that message with others. It does require that, in the earlier part of chapter 3, it is the Holy Spirit that's moving within us. It's not self-generating, but it is God that is at work in us, who moves us out, moves us forward to share this life-changing message of the gospel. And so remember that even though we are frail, sometimes when we put ourselves down and feel we're not capable, God can use us to share the message of the gospel. Sometimes we're caught up in our own selves so much that we don't move forward. God does the work in and through us.

3. WE ARE DESIGNED FOR SERVICE
(2 Cor 4:16–18; cf. 2 Cor 4:5; Mark 10:45)

The apostle Paul notes, "All this is for your benefit" (v. 15). We are designated and designed for service. Our focus is to be on things that are eternal. What things are eternal? The word and God are eternal, but so are people. Grounded in Scripture, we serve others. We look beyond ourselves. Our aim is not to be "Crazy Rich Asians" or crazy middle-class Asians. That's not our emphasis and goal. Our emphasis is really to be who God has made us to be: servants of the Lord. And in the early part of the chapter, he says, "What we preach is not ourselves, but Jesus Christ as Lord, and ourselves as your servants for Jesus' sake" (v. 5). We become servants to others, like Jesus who did not come to be served but to serve and live sacrificially (Mark 10:45).

We easily get wrapped up in ourselves. We need to pay attention to others. One thing I have learned in pastoral ministry and working with students is that everybody is hurting. We're all struggling with something. It's common to ask somebody, "How are you doing?" But if you ask, "How are you REALLY doing?" maybe that would open up an even deeper and richer conversation. See how the Lord is working in our lives, so that it saves us from ourselves. That is part of the gospel. It moves us from focusing on ourselves to give us a heart concern for others.

I know that many of us can sacrifice so much that we can, in a sense, lose ourselves. I once asked a person, "What do you want?" This person said, "I want what my friends want." Yes, that's important,